Room at the Table

A Collection of Recipes from the Premier Bed and Breakfasts of Kentucky

KEEP ON COOKIN'!

ROBIN VICTOR GOETZ

12/2011

13-digit International Standard Book Number 978-1-934898-00-0
Library of Congress Card Catalog Number 2008920805

Cover design and book layout by Asher Graphics
Photographs by Robin Victor Goetz, M.Photog.Cr.
Manufactured in China

Recipes compiled by Marsha Burton, Nancy Hinchliff, Cindy McDavid,
Devona Porter, Carol Stenbro, and Nancy Swartzel
Committee Chair and Food Stylist: Marsha Burton
Committee Vice Chair and Food Stylist: Nancy Swartzel
Editor and Food Styling Assistant: Nancy Hinchliff
Editor and Technical Support Chair: Cindy McDavid
Food Styling Assistant: Devona Porter
Food Styling Assistant: Carol Stenbro

All recipes were submitted as originals from the respective inns
and BBAK is not responsible for typographical errors and/or
checking recipes for originality.

All book order correspondence should be addressed to:

McClanahan Publishing House, Inc.
P.O. Box 100
Kuttawa, KY 42055

270-388-9388
800-544-6959
270-388-6186 FAX

www.kybooks.com

The Bed and Breakfast Association of Kentucky is a non-profit statewide association of quality inspected and approved bed and breakfast inns. Our members are dedicated to providing guests with gracious hospitality and all uphold the highest standards of comfort, cleanliness, safety, and service. Whether you are a first time guest seeking a wonderful alternative to standard hotels or a seasoned bed and breakfast traveler looking for new favorites, we represent the finest lodging choices throughout Kentucky. By requiring all of our members to be quality inspected and approved, you can travel with confidence as you experience establishments ranging from classic mansions and historic inns to quaint log cabins and rural farm settings. Each destination warmly welcomes you to relax and enjoy their quality accommodations, culinary creations, and distinctive amenities.

Contact www.kentuckybb.com for more information.

Table of Contents

* NORTHERN KY B+B

1823 Historic Rose Hill Inn

Alder and Gill Blackburn, Innkeepers
233 Rose Hill
Versailles, Kentucky 40383
800-307-0460 (toll free), 859-873-5957
Website: www.rosehillinn.com

Rose Hill Inn, one of Kentucky's finest bed and breakfasts, is only 15 minutes west of Lexington, in Versailles. Built in 1823, the historic home has been wonderfully renovated with features of the original mansion preserved and enhanced.

In 2007, Rose Hill Inn was voted "Kentucky's Best Bed and Breakfast" by readers of *Kentucky Monthly* magazine for the second year in a row. It was voted as #2 "Best Breakfast in the Southeast" and in the top 3% of all bed and breakfasts in North America in 2006 by readers of *Inn Traveler* magazine.

The charming inn is near horse farms, Keeneland Race Course, Kentucky Horse Park, and other attractions suitable for vacation, adventure, business, and family travel. It's a frequent choice for honeymoons, romantic getaways, family reunions, and meeting with old friends.

Pistachio-Crusted Pork

3/4 cup shelled pistachios
1 pork tenderloin, trimmed and cut
  crosswise into 3/4-inch thick slices
1/2 teaspoon salt
1/4 teaspoon black pepper
2 tablespoons olive oil, divided
1/2 to 3/4 cup heavy cream

Pulse pistachios in a food processor until chopped, then transfer to shallow bowl. Pat pork slices dry and sprinkle both sides with salt and pepper. Dip both sides of each slice in chopped nuts to coat, pressing to help them adhere. Heat approximately 1 tablespoon oil in a 12-inch non-stick skillet over moderate heat until hot but not smoking, then cook half of the pork slices, turning over once until browned and just cooked through. Transfer to clean plate and keep warm. Wipe out skillet and repeat with remaining slices and additional oil. Add cream to skillet and deglaze by boiling, stirring and scraping up brown bits, until reduced by half. Season with salt and pepper and pour over the pork. This dish is wonderful served with mashed potatoes and a fresh vegetable.

Yield: 4 servings.

Apricot Oatmeal Cookies

2 sticks butter, softened
1 cup light brown sugar
3/4 cup white sugar
2 eggs
1 1/2 cups all-purpose flour
1 1/2 teaspoons kosher salt
1 teaspoon baking powder
1/4 teaspoon freshly ground nutmeg
3 cups rolled oats
1 1/2 cups dried apricots
  (cranberries or raisins work well too)

In the bowl of an electric mixer or by hand, beat the butter until creamy, then add sugars and beat until fluffy, about 3 minutes with an electric mixer. Beat in eggs one at a time.

Sift together the flour, salt, baking powder, and nutmeg. Add to the butter mixture and stir to blend with a wooden spoon or large rubber spatula. Stir in oats and dried fruit.

Form dough into 1-inch balls and place on a baking sheet covered with waxed paper or parchment paper (both of which make clean-up easier, but are not required to make the cookies). Bake at 350 degrees for approximately 12 minutes, until the bottom edges turn brown. The cookies will still be soft and feel a bit undercooked at this point. If using baking paper, slide off onto a cooling rack. Otherwise, allow cookies to cool for 2 minutes on the baking sheet and then remove to the rack. Allow cookies to cool for at least 30 minutes before serving.

Yield: 48 cookies.

Creamy Tomato Soup

Prep: 30 minutes

1/2 cup olive oil, divided
1 large yellow onion, chopped
1 whole head garlic, peeled and minced
1 cup chicken stock
2 (28-ounce) cans chopped tomatoes, drained
1 large eggplant, peeled and
  cut into 1/2-inch thick slices
Salt to taste
Black pepper to taste
2 cups heavy cream
1 cup grated Asiago cheese, optional

Heat 2 tablespoons of the olive oil in stockpot. Add the onion and garlic and sauté until tender and translucent. Add chicken stock and tomatoes; simmer on low heat for 30 minutes.

Place the eggplant slices in the bottom of a pie pan and coat with 3 tablespoons of the olive oil. Bake at 450 degrees until the slices are soft. Purée the slices with remaining olive oil and add to the tomato mixture. Continue to simmer and season with the salt and pepper. Add the cream just before serving. To serve, ladle the soup into bowls. Top with grated Asiago cheese, if desired.

Yield: 8 to 10 servings.

1840 Tucker House
Bed and Breakfast

Devona and Steve Porter, Innkeepers
2406 Tucker Station Road
Louisville, Kentucky 40299
888-297-8007 (toll free), 502-297-8007
Website: www.tuckerhouse1840.com

Kentucky is world-renowned for its hospitality and cuisine, and 1840 Tucker House Bed and Breakfast is a prime example of both. Once the residence for an 825-acre farm in rural eastern Jefferson County (Louisville), it is now an elegant and gracious bed and breakfast, set on five acres of woods, meadow, gardens, and pond. While still retaining its rural feel, 1840 Tucker House is conveniently located in Louisville's east end, close to interstates, shopping, and restaurants, but only twenty minutes from the heart of downtown.

This National Register, Federal-style home is faithfully restored to its simple beauty and authentically furnished with period antiques. In addition to enjoying luxurious rooms and private baths, guests may relax on the porches or patios, explore the woods, discover the old springhouse or the slave cemetery, or even take a dip in the modern in-ground pool.

Breakfast is special at 1840 Tucker House where guests dine on antique china in the formal dining room, or on historic Kentucky Bybee pottery in the sunlit gathering room or on the adjoining deck. A "Kentucky-gourmet" breakfast is prepared in a reproduction 1840 kitchen which, at first blush, only shows an old farm sink, a cooking fireplace, soapstone and cherry countertops, and painted cabinets. Hidden behind the cabinet doors, however, are all the modern conveniences and appliances a gourmet chef needs.

Each of the four bedrooms, or "chambers" as they were called in 1840, is distinctive with luxury linens, antique furnishings, and exquisite reproduction lighting. The second-floor common room provides freshly-brewed coffee each morning, snacks, complimentary beverages, maps, menus from local restaurants, and guidebooks for local exploring.

For a relaxing weekend getaway, a country holiday, or a business trip, innkeepers Devona and Steve love to share their home where nature, history, and tranquility co-exist.

Cherry Almond Scones

Prep time: 15 minutes

1/2 cup chopped or snipped, dried cherries
2 cups all-purpose flour
1/4 cup sugar
2 teaspoons baking powder
1/4 teaspoon salt
6 tablespoons butter, cut into 1/2-inch pieces
1/3 cup almond paste, broken into small pieces
1/2 cup whole milk
1/4 teaspoon almond extract
1 egg, beaten
Marmalade, honey, or cherry preserves

Lightly spray cookie sheet or cooking stone with nonstick cooking spray. Reconstitute cherries in enough boiling water to cover the cherries. Drain well and pat dry. Set aside.

Lightly spoon flour into measuring cup and level off. In large bowl, combine flour, sugar, baking powder, and salt. Whisk together to mix. With pastry blender or two knives, cut in the butter until mixture resembles coarse crumbs. Crumble in almond paste and cut in as you did with the butter. This mixture will contain some "clumps" and the consistency will be coarser than it was before the addition of the almond paste.

In a small bowl, combine milk, almond extract, and egg. Blend well. Make a "well" in the center of the flour mixture and pour the liquid ingredients into the center. Mix with a fork just until all of the dry ingredients are moistened.

Add reconstituted dried cherries to the dough and mix in with fork. Mixture will be a bit sticky.

On a floured pastry cloth or board, scrape the dough and coat with the flour by rolling the dough on the surface gently. Knead very gently about six times; handling the dough too much will result in tougher scones.

Divide the dough in half, using a serrated-edged knife. Shape each half into a ball. Pat each ball into a 5-inch round, with the center higher than the edges. Cut each round, with a pizza cutter, into 6 wedges and place 1-inch apart on the prepared baking sheet or stone.

Bake at 400 degrees for 12 to 15 minutes or until light golden brown. Cool for 10 minutes before serving. Serve with marmalade, honey, or cherry preserves. These freeze beautifully. When ready to serve from freezer, thaw, wrap in a paper towel, and microwave for approximately 15 seconds. They will taste as if you just took them out of the oven!

Yield: 12 servings.

Two-Pepper Frittata

Prep time: 45 minutes

3 cloves garlic, minced
1 large purple onion, sliced
2 sweet red peppers, julienned
1 yellow pepper, julienned
3 tablespoons olive oil, divided
2 yellow squash, thinly sliced
2 zucchini, thinly sliced
1/2 pound fresh mushrooms, sliced
6 large eggs
1/4 cup whipping cream
2 1/2 to 3 teaspoons salt
2 teaspoons freshly ground pepper
8 slices sandwich bread,
  cubed and divided
1 (8-ounce) package cream cheese
2 cups shredded Gruyère cheese

In a large skillet over medium-high heat, cook the first four ingredients in 1 tablespoon of the olive oil until tender. Drain and pat dry; set aside. In the same skillet, cook squash and zucchini over medium-high heat in 1 tablespoon of the olive oil. Drain and pat dry; set aside. In the same skillet, cook mushrooms over medium-high heat in remaining 1 tablespoon olive oil until just tender and golden. Drain and set aside.

Whisk together eggs and next 3 ingredients in a large bowl; stir in vegetables, half of the bread cubes, cream cheese, and Gruyère. Press remaining bread cubes in the bottom of a lightly greased 10-inch springform pan and place on a baking sheet. Pour vegetable mixture into pan and bake at 325 degrees for approximately 1 hour, covering with aluminum foil after 45 minutes to prevent excessive browning. Serve warm.

Yield: 8 servings.

Raspberry Gorgonzola Salad

Dressing:

1 cup olive oil
1/2 cup raspberry vinegar
1/4 cup honey
1 teaspoon poppy seeds
1 teaspoon dried mint
1/2 teaspoon dried mustard
1/2 teaspoon salt or to taste

Salad:

3 cups shredded red cabbage
8 cups torn Bibb lettuce
8 cups mixed salad greens
1 sweet red pepper, cut into julienne strips
1/2 pint container raspberries
8-ounces Gorgonzola cheese, crumbled

Spiced pecans:

1/4 cup and 2 tablespoons sugar, divided
1 cup very hot water
1/2 tablespoon chili powder
1/8 teaspoon cayenne pepper
1 cup pecan halves

To make dressing, place olive oil, raspberry vinegar, honey, poppy seeds, mint, mustard, and salt in a jar with a tight-fitting lid; shake well to combine.

To make the salad, first shred the red cabbage by cutting the head into quarters. Then place a quarter section with a cut side down on the cutting board. Hold a chef knife perpendicular to the cabbage. Slice it into 1/4-inch thick shreds. Marinate the cabbage in 1 cup of the dressing for one hour in the refrigerator. You can marinate it longer, if necessary; it keeps in the refrigerator up to one week. Next wash the Bibb lettuce and the greens. Dry and place in a large salad bowl. Keep the bowl in the refrigerator until ready to serve.

To prepare the spiced pecans, in a medium bowl stir together 1/4 cup sugar and hot water until the sugar dissolves. Add pecan halves and soak for 10 minutes. Drain, discarding sugar mixture. Combine 2 tablespoons sugar, chili powder, and cayenne pepper. Add pecans, tossing to coat. Place on a baking sheet lined with Silpat™ or parchment paper. Bake at 350 degrees for 10 minutes, remove from oven and stir. Bake for an additional 5 to 10 minutes or until pecans are deep golden brown.

To serve, drain the cabbage and reserve the dressing. Toss the lettuce with enough of the dressing to coat the greens. Arrange the salad on individual plates. Top with the red cabbage, red pepper strips, and the raspberries. Sprinkle with the crumbled Gorgonzola cheese.

Yield: 12 servings.

Whole Wheat Herb Bread

2 packages dry yeast
1/2 cup warm water (105° to 115°)
1/4 cup and 1 tablespoon honey, divided
3 cups whole milk, divided
1/4 cup and 1 tablespoon olive oil
2 tablespoons butter
6 cups unbleached flour
3 cups whole wheat flour
   (preferably stone-ground)
1 1/2 teaspoons salt
1 teaspoon dried basil
1 teaspoon dried oregano
1 teaspoon celery flakes
1 teaspoon onion flakes
1/2 teaspoon dried thyme
1 teaspoon dried parsley flakes
1/2 teaspoon dried sage
1 teaspoon dried rosemary

In a measuring container that will hold at least 2 cups, dissolve the yeast in warm water, stir in 1 tablespoon honey, and set aside. The mixture will rise and bubble out of a smaller container!

In a medium-sized, heavy saucepan, combine 2 cups whole milk, olive oil, 1/4 cup honey, butter, and all of the dried herbs. Heat slowly to about 105 degrees. If the mixture becomes too hot, cool it with the reserved 1 cup milk. You will want to have all 3 cups of the milk in the mixture.

Remove the mixture from the stove and stir in the yeast mixture, which should be bubbly by now. (The addition of the honey to the yeast/water mixture proofs the yeast so that you know the yeast is active.)

Combine the flours and salt (do not forget or forego the salt) in a very large mixing bowl; whisk until combined thoroughly. Add the milk mixture and stir until all ingredients are moistened. It is best to stir with your clean hands; the dough will be very sticky and a spoon doesn't work particularly well!

Turn the dough out onto a heavily floured surface, and knead 4 to 6 minutes or until the dough is smooth and elastic. Place the dough in a well-greased bowl, turning to grease the top (I use butter for this.) Cover with a clean cloth and let the dough rise in a warm place, free from drafts, about 50 minutes or until the dough has doubled in bulk.

Punch the dough down and turn out onto a floured surface. Let the dough rest for 5 minutes. Then knead the dough 3 or 4 times by turning and folding dough under itself, adding flour as needed.

Divide the dough into thirds. Shape each third into a loaf by rolling it into a long rectangle and then, starting at the short end, continue rolling and sealing the dough. Flatten and fold the ends under the loaf. Place loaves in three greased loaf pans. Cover and let rise in a warm place, free from drafts, approximately 30 minutes or until doubled in size. It is important not to let the loaves rise too much!

Meanwhile, preheat the oven to 350 degrees. When the loaves have risen, bake them for 40 to 45 minutes or until they sound hollow when tapped. (You can cover them with foil the last few minutes, if necessary, to keep them from browning too much.) Remove the loaves from the oven and let cool on racks for about 15 minutes; then remove the loaves from the pans onto wire racks until the bread is cool enough to slice. Take your bows and enjoy!

Yield: 3 hearty loaves.

Aebleskiver

Prep time: 30 minutes

2 cups all-purpose flour
1 teaspoon baking soda
1 teaspoon baking powder
3 to 4 tablespoons sugar
1 teaspoon salt, optional
1 tablespoon cardamom
4 eggs, separated
1 teaspoon vanilla extract
1/2 cup (1 stick) butter, melted
1 3/4 cups buttermilk
Butter for frying
Chopped apples, raisins, jam,
**   caramel, berries, chocolate, etc.**
**   for filling**
Confectioners' sugar to taste

Aebleskiver are traditional Danish spherical pancakes, cooked in a special pan available online or in specialty shops.

In a large bowl, mix the dry ingredients (flour, baking soda, baking powder, sugar, salt, and cardamom) together. In a separate bowl, mix the egg yolks, vanilla extract, and melted butter together. In another bowl, beat the egg whites until they are foamy and can hold a soft peak. Add the buttermilk to the flour mixture and mix lightly—like pancake batter. Some lumps are okay. Add the egg and butter mixture into the batter and then gently fold in the egg whites.

Place about a 1/2 teaspoon butter into each of the hollows of the pan and pour the batter into the hollows, about 2/3 full. Add a berry or a dollop of jam, caramel, or chocolate (whatever you like) to the center of each aebleskive, then add a little more batter to cover the filling item. Try not to overfill!

Place the aebleskiver pan over a medium heat until it is good and hot, about 390 degrees.

When the bottom is browned lightly, use a pair of wooden skewers to gently turn the aebleskiver, then turn them frequently to form a ball. They should be light and airy—a cross between a waffle and a pancake.

Place on paper towels in a warm oven (200 degrees) or a warming drawer until ready to serve. Sprinkle with confectioners' sugar just before serving.

Yield: 45 small aebleskiver.

Butternut Squash Bourbon Bisque

Prep time: 40 minutes

2 medium-size butternut squash
2 tablespoons extra-virgin olive oil
1 cup diced onions
1 cup chopped leeks
1 teaspoon ground cumin
2 tablespoons minced garlic
1 tablespoon chopped fresh ginger root
4 tablespoons pure maple syrup
2 tablespoons soy sauce
1/4 cup bourbon
1/2 cup dry sherry
1/4 teaspoon freshly grated nutmeg
5 cups roasted chicken stock
1 cup whipping cream
Salt to taste
Freshly ground white pepper to taste
2 tablespoons cornstarch and water mix
Chives and sour cream for garnish

Slice the squash in half lengthwise, place in a shallow baking dish lined with aluminum foil, cut side down, and roast at 375 degrees for about 1 hour, or until the squash is soft when you push on it. Let squash cool enough to be handled. Peel, seed, and remove strings. Cut the roasted squash into 1-inch pieces or scoop "meat" out with a sturdy spoon.

In a large heavy stock pot, heat the olive oil and add the onions. Cook until onions are translucent. Add the leeks and cumin and cook for an additional 2 to 3 minutes. Add the garlic and ginger and cook until the garlic is fragrant and the onions are a light golden color. Add the maple syrup, soy sauce, bourbon, sherry, and nutmeg and stir together. Add the squash and the chicken stock (you may use homemade chicken stock for added flavor, if desired) and bring just to the boiling point. Lower the heat and cook gently for about 15 to 25 minutes.

Using an immersion blender (or a regular blender with small amounts at a time) purée until very smooth. Add the whipping cream, salt, and pepper. Cook for 2 minutes to heat through. Do not boil. Add cornstarch mixture to soup. To serve, ladle in soup bowls and garnish with fresh snipped chives and a dollop of sour cream.

Yield: 6 servings.

Roasted Baby Beets

5 bunches baby beets,
   approximately 1 inch in diameter
5 large, fresh rosemary sprigs
2 tablespoons butter
1/4 cup extra-virgin olive oil
Salt to taste
White pepper to taste
Additional rosemary sprigs for garnish

Wash beets, trim the tops, and place in a shallow roasting pan. Add rosemary sprigs. Add water to the pan, just enough to lightly cover the beets. Roast beets, covered with aluminum foil, at 375 degrees until tender, approximately 30 to 40 minutes. Remove the skin from the beets while they are still warm. Transfer beets to a rimmed baking sheet, cover, and chill. Beets can be chilled for up to 1 day before proceeding to the next step.

In a small saucepan, melt the butter and olive oil. Toss the beets with the mixture, add salt and pepper to taste, and then return the beets to the baking sheet. Bake at 350 degrees, stirring occasionally, until thoroughly heated, approximately 15 to 25 minutes. To serve, place beets in a serving dish and garnish with rosemary sprigs.

Yield: 8 to 10 servings.

1851 Historic Maple Hill Manor

Todd Allen and Tyler Horton, Owners, Innkeepers, Alpaca and Llama Breeders
2941 Perryville Road (US 150 East)
Springfield, Kentucky 40069
800-886-7546 (toll free), 859-336-3075
Website: www.maplehillmanor.com

Circa 1851, Maple Hill Manor is an award-winning bed and breakfast, alpaca and llama farm, and fiber farm store. It is listed on the National Register of Historic Places and has been designated a Kentucky Landmark Home.

Exterior walls are four rows of brick thick and interior walls are three rows thick. All the wood came from the original plantation with millwork and brick-making completed onsite. Its architectural features include 7,000 square feet, lavished in Italianate detail, 14-foot ceilings, 12-foot doorways, 9-foot windows, and a grand cherry, floating spiral staircase. Its interior gems include original Empire woodwork, 14-inch baseboards, fireplaces featured in every room, and three Italian crystal chandeliers dated 1900 and that once hung in the Grand Kentucky Hotel in downtown Louisville. A floor-to-ceiling library is filled with books and memorabilia of Abraham Lincoln whose Kentucky-pioneer grandfather and parents were local residents.

Maple Hill is well-known for its historic, antique-appointed accommodations, special events such as weddings, receptions, reunions, retreats, murder mysteries, and its champion pedigree alpacas and llamas. As a working farm, the manor is actively involved in agritourism. The Suri alpacas and llamas, extremely rare camelids from South America, produce the finest fibers used in luxury clothing as well as blankets, baby wear, hats, gloves, scarves, coats, pillows, and rugs – all of which can be purchased at their farm store and studio.

Glazed Bacon

Prep: 10 minutes

1/2 cup all-purpose flour
1/3 cup brown sugar
1 teaspoon freshly ground black pepper
1 teaspoon cinnamon, optional
1 pound thick sliced bacon

Line cookie sheet with parchment paper to keep from sticking. Combine flour, sugar, and spices in a gallon zip top bag. Add bacon, a few pieces at a time, and shake to coat well. Place bacon on the cookie sheet so they are not touching each other. After baking, place on paper towels to drain. Bake at 300 degrees for approximately 30 to 40 minutes.

Yield: 8 servings.

Rosemary Garlic Pork Tenderloin

3 1/2 to 4 pounds pork loin
Olive oil for drizzling
1 tablespoon garlic salt
3 to 4 tablespoons Rosemary Garlic seasoning
4 sprigs fresh rosemary, cut or chopped

Coat a large baking pan with cooking spray. Drizzle pork loin with olive oil and massage all sides with garlic salt and Rosemary Garlic seasoning. Add fresh rosemary. Cover with aluminum foil and bake, fat side up, at 375 degrees for 1 hour and 30 minutes or until core temperature reaches 160 to 165 degrees. To serve, slice and garnish with fresh rosemary.

Yield: 6 to 8 servings.

1853 Inn at Woodhaven

Marsha Burton, Innkeeper
401 South Hubbards Lane
Louisville, Kentucky 40207
888-895-1011 (toll free), 502-895-1011
Website: www.innatwoodhaven.com

Auntie Pankie's Garlic Cheese Grits

1 cup Weisenberger stone-ground grits
  or quality stone-ground grits
4 cups boiling water
1 teaspoon salt
1 stick butter
6-ounce roll Kraft garlic cheese
1 egg, beaten
3/4 cup milk
Dash of hot sauce
1 cup grated sharp Cheddar
  or Parmesan cheese
3 large shrimp per person, sautéed and
  placed on a small wood skewer to garnish

Welcome to the Inn at Woodhaven, a Gothic Revival mansion conveniently located near many of Louisville's finest attractions, restaurants, and shopping venues. Built in 1853 and listed on the National Register of Historic Places, the mansion's original features have been skillfully maintained to include elaborately carved woodwork, grand porches, winding staircases, ceiling plaster detail, diamond windowpanes with trefoil decorations, interior shutters, and magnificent 14-foot arched gothic doors.

At this historic inn, guests discover pampering touches around every corner. Expansive common areas offer books, magazines, after dinner liquors, and fresh cookies. Relaxing rooms are found in the Main House, Carriage House, or the award-winning and romantic Rose Cottage. Elegant guest rooms are decorated with period antiques and reproductions plus in room amenities including luxurious linens and bath towels, exclusive bath products, televisions with DVD players, wireless Internet, refrigerators, and complimentary stations featuring coffee, tea, and snacks. Several rooms also boast whirlpool spa tubs, steam showers, and cozy fireplaces. In-room massages are available in any guest room.

Woodhaven's renowned breakfast features organic fruits and juices, cage-free eggs, local pastries, organic bacon and sausage, pancakes, caramel French toast, and biscuits and gravy. The dining room is furnished with separate tables, white tablecloths and napkins, and fine china. Fresh flowers, flickering candlelight, and soft music enhance the dining experience. For those who like to linger in their room, breakfast may be ordered and is then delivered in a festive basket.

In Louisville, Woodhaven provides exceptional hospitality and beautiful surroundings.

Cook grits in boiling salted water until thick. Remove from heat and stir in butter and cheese roll. Mix egg, milk, and Tabasco together and then add to grits. Pour grits into a buttered 2-quart casserole dish, top with Cheddar or Parmesan cheese, and bake at 350 degrees for 1 hour. To serve, garnish with shrimp skewers.

Yield: 8 servings.

Sweet Corn Sauté

3 large ears sweet corn
1 medium red bell pepper,
  cut in half with stem and ribs removed
1 medium poblano pepper,
  cut in half with stem and ribs removed
1 medium red onion, peeled and halved
4 tablespoons olive oil, divided
Salt to taste
Pepper to taste
2 tablespoons fresh lime juice
2 tablespoons honey
1/3 cup chopped fresh cilantro

Prepare a charcoal grill or preheat the broiler. Brush the corn, peppers, and onion with 3 tablespoons of the oil and salt and pepper generously. Place the vegetables on a medium hot grill or baking sheet. Cook or broil on all sides until they just begin to show color. Remove and cool. When cool, cut the kernels from the corn. Pull as much of the skin as possible off the peppers, dice, and then add to the corn. Dice the onion and add to the corn along with the lime juice, honey, cilantro, and remaining olive oil. Let sit for at least 30 minutes or it can be stored in the refrigerator for up to three days.

Yield: 10 servings.

Tenderloin of Beef and Blackberry Sauce

Tenderloin:

1 pound beef tenderloin, trimmed
Garlic olive oil
Salt to taste
Freshly cracked black pepper to taste

Sauce:

1 (12-ounce) bottle chili sauce
1 (14-ounce) bottle ketchup
1 (5-ounce) bottle Worcestershire sauce
1 (12-ounce) bottle Major Grey Indian
 curry sauce
1 (10-ounce) bottle of A.1. steak sauce
1 cup seedless blackberry jam
2 large garlic heads, baked
Fresh blackberries to garnish

Place tenderloin in a roasting pan, coat with oil, and sprinkle with salt and pepper. Roast tenderloin at 400 degrees until meat thermometer reads 130 degrees for medium rare, about 35 minutes. Cool for 10 minutes and then slice. This can be cooked the day before and refrigerated. When ready to serve, bring to room temperature.

To prepare the sauce, mix all ingredients together and store in the refrigerator. Add fresh blackberries to garnish. Serve with Sweet Corn Sauté and Roasted Red Bell Pepper Sauce.

Yield: 8 to 12 servings.

Roasted Red Bell Pepper Sauce

Olive oil
3 large red bell peppers
1 tablespoon roasted garlic
1/2 cup chicken broth
Salt to taste
Pepper to taste
1/2 teaspoon chopped chipotle in
 adobo or hot sauce
Butter, optional

Lightly oil the peppers and arrange on a baking sheet. Roast at 450 degrees until the skins are blistered. Remove from the oven and place in a bowl; cover with plastic wrap and allow peppers to steam for a few minutes. Scrap the skins off the peppers and discard the skin, seeds, and stems. Transfer to a blender or food processor, add the garlic and purée until smooth. Add broth to thin the sauce to desired consistency. Season with salt, pepper, and the chipotle or hot sauce. Serve warm with the tenderloin of beef. If adding butter, stir in just before serving. Can be made up to three days in advance and stored in the refrigerator.

Yield: 10 servings.

Noodles Louise

1 (5-ounce) package angel hair
   pasta
1 cup cottage cheese
1 cup sour cream
2 cloves garlic, chopped fine
1 medium onion, chopped fine
1 tablespoon Worcestershire
   sauce
Dash of Tabasco
Salt to taste
Pepper to taste
1/2 cup grated
   Parmesan cheese

   Cook pasta according to package directions and drain well. Combine pasta and all remaining ingredients, except the Parmesan cheese, and mix thoroughly. Pour the mixture into a well-greased casserole dish and sprinkle the Parmesan cheese evenly over top. Bake at 350 degrees for 45 minutes.

   Yield: 8 servings.

Woodford Pudding

Pudding:

1 cup butter, melted and cooled
6 eggs
1 cup buttermilk
2 cups Windstone Farm blackberry jam,
  preferably seedless
2 cups sugar
2 cups all-purpose flour
2 teaspoons baking soda
2 teaspoons cinnamon

Sauce:

2 cups brown sugar
2 cups cream
2 sticks butter
Glug glug of Woodford Reserve bourbon

Mix butter, eggs, and buttermilk in a large bowl; stir in jam. Combine dry ingredients and add to liquid, mix until creamy. Pour into a greased 9 x 13-inch pan or large bunt pan. Bake at 350 degrees for 45 minutes or until pudding is set.

In a saucepan, combine brown sugar and cream and bring to a boil, stirring constantly. Add butter and whisk until blended; add bourbon. Pour sauce over warm cake, setting some extra aside for drizzling when served.

Yield: 12 servings.

Race Day Pie

1 cup semisweet chocolate chips
1 (9-inch) unbaked pie shell
1/2 cup finely chopped pecans
3/4 cup white sugar
3/4 cup white corn syrup
3 eggs, slightly beaten
1/2 stick butter, melted
1 teaspoon vanilla extract
1/4 cup bourbon, optional

Layer chocolate chips in bottom of pie shell and layer pecans on top. In a medium bowl, mix sugar, white corn syrup, and eggs until well blended. Add melted butter, vanilla extract, and bourbon and blend again. Pour mixture over chocolate chips and pecans and bake at 350 degrees for 45 minutes or until almost set. Pie will become firm as it cools.

Yield: 8 servings.

Honey-Bourbon Pork Tenderloin with Sautéed Maple Apples and Wild Mushrooms

(pictured on page 22)

Prep: 40 to 50 minutes

1/2 cup diced onions
1/2 cup lemon juice
1/2 cup bourbon
1/2 cup honey
1/4 cup low sodium soy sauce
2 tablespoons olive oil
4 garlic cloves, minced
3 (3/4 pound) pork tenderloins
1/2 teaspoon salt
1/4 teaspoon freshly cracked black pepper
6 1/2 cups assorted whole mushrooms
1 tablespoon butter
1 tablespoon olive oil
Salt to taste
Pepper to taste
4 large Granny Smith apples, peeled,
   cored, and sliced thin into apple rings
1 tablespoon butter, melted
4 tablespoons maple syrup
3 tablespoons all-purpose flour
1 1/4 cups water

Combine first 7 ingredients in a large zip-lock bag and add the tenderloins. Seal and place in the refrigerator for 30 minutes. Remove tenderloins from bag, reserving marinade. Sprinkle meat with salt and pepper. Place tenderloins in a broiler pan coated with cooking spray. Insert meat thermometer into thickest part of the pork. Bake at 425 degrees for 25 minutes or until meat reaches 160 degrees (slightly pink), basting once with the marinade. Let cooked tenderloin rest for 5 minutes, then cut into slices and cover with aluminum foil to keep warm.

While pork is cooking, sauté mushrooms in butter and olive oil over medium heat for 10 minutes. Season with salt and pepper. Remove from heat and set aside.

Next sauté apple rings in a skillet with melted butter over medium-high heat for 5 minutes, turning once. Add maple syrup and simmer for 12 minutes or until apples are tender. Set aside.

Place flour in saucepan. Gradually add remaining marinade, water and any pan drippings, stirring with a whisk until blended. Bring to a boil over medium-high heat and cook for 3 minutes or until the mixture reaches desired thickness, stirring constantly.

To serve, place 2 warm apple rings on each plate. Arrange pork slices on top, spoon mushrooms and sauce over pork.

Yield: 6 servings.

Woodhaven Dill Bread

3 cups self-rising flour
3 tablespoons light brown sugar
2 tablespoons dried dillweed
1 (12-ounce) can light beer
1/2 stick butter, melted

Grease a 9 x 5-inch loaf pan. Mix the flour, brown sugar, and dillweed. Add the beer and mix well. Pour the batter into the greased loaf pan. Pour the butter over the batter and bake at 375 degrees for 55 minutes. Turn out onto a cooling rack. Leftovers are great toasted and topped with a poached egg.

Yield: 1 loaf.

LEXINGTON
26 MILES
PLEASANT HILL
MILES
HARRODSBURG
7 MILES
PERRYVILLE
17 MILES

1869 Shaker Tavern

Jo Ann Moody, Innkeeper
U.S. 73
South Union, Kentucky 42283
800-929-8701 (toll free), 270-542-6801
Website: www.shakermuseum.com

The Shaker Tavern, built in 1869 as a business venture for the South Union Shakers, housed a hotel for the "people of the world." The Shakers leased the building to an outside interest for one hundred dollars a month, leaving its management to the "world."

The tavern maintained a thriving business for more than forty years, catering to the Victorian railroad travelers who stopped at South Union. The building's architectural features were clearly incorporated to attract the world's people, whose tastes differed dramatically from that of the Shakers. The stark simplicity of the buildings contrasts greatly with the grand columned facade, intricate brickwork, and the ornate staircase.

The Shaker Tavern is owned and operated by the Shaker Museum at South Union.

Shaker Lemon Pie

2 large or 3 medium-size juicy lemons, clean well
2 cups sugar
4 eggs
2 pie crusts

Cut lemons into paper thin slices, then quarter the slices. Remove seeds and end slices. Layer slices in a bowl and sprinkle with sugar. Cover and let sit several hours or overnight.

Place one pie crust in a 9-inch pie plate. Lift lemons out of sugar and layer in crust. Sprinkle with a little more sugar if you wish. Add eggs to sugar/lemon juice and beat until well blended. Pour over lemon slices. Top with remaining crust and crimp the edges to seal. Cut slits in the top to vent for steam. Bake at 375 degrees until golden brown, approximately 45 minutes.

Yield: 8 to 10 servings.

Bourbon Sweet Potato Casserole

Potatoes:

3 cups mashed sweet potatoes
1 cup sugar
1 stick butter, melted
2 eggs, beaten
1 teaspoon vanilla extract
1/3 cup milk
1 to 1 1/4 teaspoons Maker's Mark bourbon

Topping:

1/2 cup brown sugar
1/4 cup all-purpose flour
1/4 cup or less butter, softened
1/2 cup chopped pecans

Combine the first 7 ingredients with a mixer and pour into a 2-quart baking dish. Mix topping ingredients together and sprinkle on top of the sweet potatoes. Bake at 350 degrees until bubbly, approximately 20 minutes.

Yield: 12 servings.

Aleksander House
Bed and Breakfast

Nancy Hinchliff, Innkeeper
1213 South First Street
Louisville, Kentucky 40203
886-637-4985 (toll free), 502-637-4985
Website: www.aleksanderhouse.com

The Aleksander House Bed and Breakfast is a gracious, 1882 Victorian home, centrally located in historic Old Louisville, the third largest preservation area in the country. Near shops, restaurants, museums and many other attractions, the three-story brick building is listed on the National Registry of Historic Landmarks.

Built by Charles A Hemphill, the first president of the Presbyterian Seminary, the Aleksander House was restored in the early 1990s, and retains 14-foot ceilings, original hardwood floors, light fixtures, stained glass, and fireplaces. Five spacious guest rooms are tastefully decorated in eclectic or traditional furnishings.

Breakfast at the Aleksander House is a real treat. It may consist of Belgian waffles, French toast, Dutch apple pancakes, or one of many savory egg dishes, such as vegetable and cheese quiches, croissants au gratin, or eggs Benedict.

Aleksander House Mint Juleps
(pictured on page 113)

Simple Syrup:

2 cups water
2 cups sugar
8 sprigs mint leaves

Mint Juleps:

Kentucky Colonel Spearmint Leaves, large handful
Ice, finely crushed
Derby glasses or silver mugs
Maker's Mark bourbon, up to 32 ounces
Straws, cut to about one inch above glass or mug

To prepare simple syrup, combine water and sugar in a small saucepan and boil 5 minutes. Pour into storage container. Add mint leaves, cover, and let steep overnight.

To prepare the Mint Juleps, place 1 to 2 ounces of simple syrup into glass or mug. Add a sprig of mint and crush with a wooden spoon. Fill glass with finely crushed ice. Pour 1 to 2 ounces of bourbon over ice.

Garnish with a sprig of fresh spearmint, add a short straw and serve.

Yield: 32 servings
(serving size: 1 ounce simple syrup and
1 ounce bourbon).

Fresh Baby Greens with Chicken, Mango, Yellow Bell Pepper, and Goat Cheese

Prep: 10 minutes (salad), 10 minutes (dressing)

Salad:

4 cups spring greens
1 yellow bell pepper, chopped
1 cup grape tomatoes, cut in half
1/2 cup shredded carrots
2 to 3 green onion springs, sliced
1 cup chopped mangos
2 baked, roasted, or fried chicken breasts,
   cut into bite-size pieces
1 small avocado,
   chopped and sprinkled with lime juice

Dressing:

1/4 cup olive oil
Juice of 1 1/2 limes
1 tablespoon wine vinegar (red or white)
Fresh basil, chopped
1 tablespoon Thai Chili Garlic Sauce
   (gourmet food market)
Goat cheese, crumbled

To prepare salad, lightly toss together first 6 ingredients, except chopped avocado, in a large salad bowl. Add chicken pieces and gently mix.

To prepare dressing, combine all ingredients, except goat cheese, in a small jar. Shake to mix thoroughly. Pour dressing over vegetables and toss thoroughly. Add chopped avocado. To serve, ladle onto individual salad plates and top with crumbled goat cheese.

Yield: 4 servings.

Grand Marnier French Toast

French Toast:

Parisian-style French bread
  (3/4 to 1-inch slices)
3 cups heavy cream
1 cup orange juice
4 eggs
4 tablespoons sugar
2 tablespoons orange zest
4 tablespoons Grand Marnier liqueur
2 tablespoons melted butter

Orange Butter:

6 ounces butter, softened
Juice of 1 orange
Zest of 1 orange
1/2 cup confectioners' sugar
1 tablespoon Grand Marnier liqueur
Mint leaves for garnish

    Put 12 to 16 pieces of bread in a large rectangle baking dish. Mix remaining ingredients and pour over bread. Put in refrigerator for several hours. Turn over and soak overnight. The next morning, preheat oven to 350 to 375 degrees. Brush rimmed cookie sheets generously with melted butter. Lay pieces of French toast onto buttered pans. Brush tops of French toast pieces with melted butter. Bake for approximately 45 minutes to an hour, turning halfway through baking time.

    To make the orange butter, mix all the ingredients together and form into a ball or mold. Garnish with mint leaves.

    To serve, remove the French toast from pans, transfer to plates, and sprinkle with confectioners' sugar. Garnish and serve two pieces to each person with orange butter and maple syrup.

    Yield: 6 to 8 servings (serving size: 2 pieces).

Tarragon Eggs in Puff Pastry

4 frozen pastry shells
4 large eggs
2 tablespoons creamy Caesar dressing
3/4 teaspoon dried tarragon
1/4 cup finely chopped ham
1/4 cup finely chopped green onion
1 to 2 tablespoons butter
Parsley sprigs for garnish

Bake pastry shells according to package directions and set aside. They may be kept warm in oven, wrapped in aluminum foil at 225 degrees, up to 20 minutes.

Whisk together eggs, dressing, and tarragon. Add ham and onion. In a large skillet, melt butter. Add egg mixture and scramble over low heat until set. Do not overcook.

Carefully remove caps from pastry shells and scoop out excess dough from inside, to make a pocket. Divide eggs among the 4 shells. Eggs will spill over. Garnish with caps from shells and a sprig of parsley. Serve with bacon and mixed fresh fruit cups.

Other variations: You may use ranch dressing instead of Caesar dressing, 1/2 teaspoon dried dill with 3/4 teaspoon dried basil instead of tarragon, and eliminate ham, if desired.

Yield: 4 servings.

Pears in White Zinfandel

8 pears
2 cups white Zinfandel
2 tablespoons lemon juice
1 cup sugar
2 teaspoons cinnamon
Zest of 1 lemon
1 teaspoon vanilla extract
Crème fraîche
Mint leaves

Peel pears and then core from the bottom up, leaving the stems intact. Set aside. In a deep saucepan, combine wine, lemon juice, sugar, cinnamon, lemon zest, and vanilla extract. Bring to a boil. Add the pears with stems up, and scoop spoonfuls of liquid over them. Simmer until pears are tender, 10 to 20 minutes. Remove pears and place in individual serving dishes. Strain liquid and boil until reduced by half. Pour wine sauce over pears and let cool. Serve with crème fraîche on the side and garnish with mint leaves.

Yield: 8 servings.

Banana Crepes

Prep time: 30 minutes

Crepes:

2 eggs
1 cup milk
3/4 cup sugar
Pinch of salt
3/4 cup all-purpose flour
6 to 8 teaspoons butter, divided
Whipped cream
Raspberries and mint leaves for garnish

Bananas:

4 tablespoons butter
1 cup packed dark brown sugar
2 ounces banana liqueur or other favorite liqueur
4 ounces dark rum
Ground cinnamon to taste
3 to 4 bananas, sliced

In a medium-size mixing bowl, whisk together eggs, milk, sugar, and salt. Add flour and beat until smooth. Let stand for 30 minutes. Melt 1 teaspoon of butter into the center of a small crepe pan or skillet and roll to cover the bottom of the pan. Pour 1/4-cup batter into the pan. Lift and turn the pan until the batter covers the bottom. Cook until lightly browned, turning to brown on the other side. Remove the crepe to a wire rack or wooden cutting block and cover with a paper towel. Repeat with remaining batter, adding butter to skillet when needed. Stack crepes with paper towels separating each crepe.

To prepare bananas, melt butter and add brown sugar. Let caramelize over medium-high heat for approximately 5 minutes. Stir in liqueur and rum. Add cinnamon and stir until warm. Add bananas. Gently stir to coat bananas with sauce. Variation: Apples, peaches or pears may be used instead of bananas.

To assemble, place two crepes on each serving plate. Ladle approximately 8 to 10 banana slices with rum sauce onto each crepe. Roll to enclose fruit and drizzle sauce over the top of each crepe. Top with whipped cream, a couple of raspberries, and a mint leaf. Serve immediately with bacon, orange juice, and coffee. Yum!

Variation: May also be served as a dessert with wine.

Yield: 4 servings (serving size: 2 crepes).

Strawberry-Lime Crush

1 pint fresh strawberries
3/4 cup orange juice
2 fresh limes, juiced
2 cups ice cubes
Sugar to taste
1/2 cup vodka, optional

Place all ingredients in a blender and process on high until smooth and well blended.

Serve in stemmed glasses. Garnish with a slice of lime.

Yield: 4 servings.

Amos Shinkle Townhouse

Bernie Moorman, Innkeeper
215 Garrard Street
Covington, Kentucky 41011
800-972-7012 (toll free), 859-431-2118
Website: www.amosshinkle.net

The Amos Shinkle Townhouse is a bed and breakfast hotel located on the riverfront in Covington, directly across the Ohio River from downtown Cincinnati.

Described by the New York Times as "...one of the most beautiful places to sleep in the Cincinnati area."

The home and carriage house have retained the beauty and grandeur of the 1880s.

Nash's Goetta Sandwich

Marinated Tomato Slices:

1 Tomato
Balsamic vinegar to taste
Olive oil to taste
Montreal steak seasoning to taste

Crisp Goetta Slices:

4 (1/4-inch) slices goetta
Oil, butter, or margarine for frying
Montreal steak seasoning to taste

Sandwich:

4 bagels or 8 slices bagel bread
8 or more tablespoons soft cream cheese
 spread, divided
Sliced green olives with pimento
Hot sauce to taste
Marinated tomato slices
Crisp goetta slices

To prepare the marinated tomatoes, slice a tomato into 4 or 5 slices and place slices into a glass baking dish. Sprinkle balsamic vinegar on tomato slices, then sprinkle olive oil on tomatoes, and next carefully sprinkle Montreal steak seasoning onto tomatoes. A little bit of seasoning goes a long way. Let tomatoes marinate at room temperature for 15 to 20 minutes.

To prepare the crisp goetta, fry slices of goetta in oil, margarine, or butter. Cook until the cooking sides are golden brown. Flip patties over in skillet. Pat the patties with a spatula until each one is flattened. Carefully and sparingly sprinkle Montreal steak seasoning on each goetta. Cook until cooking sides are golden brown.

To assemble the sandwiches, first toast the bagels. Spread approximately 1 tablespoon cream cheese onto the cut surfaces of each bagel. Place the sliced olives on the cream cheese, sprinkle on the hot sauce, place a marinated tomato on top, and then place a slice of goetta on top. Finish with the second half of each toasted bagel on top.

Yield: 4 sandwiches.

Amos Shinkle Eggs Benedict

Basic Hollandaise Sauce:

1/2 cup butter or margarine, melted and divided
4 egg yolks at room temperature, well beaten
2 or 2 1/2 tablespoons lemon juice
Pinch of white pepper
1/8 teaspoon salt
1/4 teaspoon garlic powder

Eggs Benedict:

8 slices (1/8 to 1/4-inch thick) Canadian bacon
1 tablespoon vinegar
8 eggs
English muffins
Basic Hollandaise Sauce
Orange slices for garnish
20 halved black olives for garnish
Strawberries, parsley, or mint for garnish

To prepare the hollandaise sauce, melt two tablespoons of the butter in the top of a double boiler. In a separate bowl, gradually pour the melted butter into egg yolks, stirring constantly. Return the yolks and butter to top of the double boiler. Turn off burner. Add the remaining butter one tablespoon at a time and continue to whisk. Remove from the heat and stir in the lemon juice, pepper, salt, and garlic powder. Keep the sauce warm but not directly on the burner. Keep covered until the eggs are poached and the English muffins are toasted.

To prepare the Canadian bacon, first spray a large skillet with cooking spray. Place all 8 slices of Canadian bacon in the skillet and lightly brown on both sides. Keep warm until the eggs are poached.

To prepare the poached eggs, heat 2 to 3 inches of water in a large saucepan over medium heat until almost boiling. Add 1 tablespoon vinegar. Crack eggs into small cups and slide one by one from the cups into the simmering water, cooking 4 eggs at a time. If an egg sinks to the bottom, wait until it is nearly set before attempting to dislodge with a slotted spoon. Cook until the whites are set and the centers are still soft. Remove with a slotted spoon and set in a second pot of water warmed to 150 degrees. Cover and let stand for 15 minutes. Drain each egg and trim excess edges.

To serve, toast English muffins, brush with butter, and keep warm. To assemble, place an English muffin with both halves open on each plate. Add bacon, 1 slice on each half muffin; then top each bacon slice with 1 poached egg. Ladle approximately 3 tablespoons of hollandaise sauce over each egg.

Garnish each plate with 1 orange slice, 5 halved black olives, a few strawberries, parsley or mint. Enjoy!

Yield: 4 servings.

Austin's Inn Place

Mary and Tom Austin, Innkeepers
915 South 1st Street
Louisville, Kentucky 40203
502-585-8855
Website: www.austinsinnplace.com

Beyond the traditional bed and breakfast, Austin's Inn Place is a guest and gathering bed and breakfast inn located in Old Louisville. It's located just blocks from the center of downtown, in two beautiful 1888 vintage Victorian homes. Moderately priced, the inn provides luxurious comfort and the ambience of visiting with good friends.

Elegant décor is noticed throughout the inn, which features eight guest rooms, three dining rooms, parlor, game room, party room, and bar. A fountain and lush garden enhance their off-street, gated parking.

Cherry Torte

1 (12-ounce) package frozen dark sweet cherries, thawed
1 egg
1 cup sugar
1 tablespoon butter, melted
1 teaspoon almond extract
1 cup all-purpose flour
1/2 teaspoon salt
2 teaspoons baking powder
1 teaspoon cinnamon
3/4 cup chopped pecans
2 (3-ounce) packages cream cheese
2 to 3 tablespoons milk
1 (21-ounce) can whole cherry pie filling or
   fresh cherries and blueberries

Slice the cherries into halves. In a large bowl, beat the egg. Gradually add the sugar, melted butter, and extract to the egg and beat thoroughly. Fold in the cherries. Add sifted dry ingredients and nuts to the bowl; stir until combined. Bake in a greased pie plate for 45 minutes at 350 degrees.

Blend cream cheese with milk to make a smooth sauce. Serve torte with cream cheese topping; add pie filling or fresh fruit on top of cream cheese.

Yield: 6 servings.

Ratatouille

1 medium-size eggplant, peeled and cubed
2 small zucchini, peeled and cubed
1 small green pepper, thinly sliced
1 small yellow pepper, thinly sliced
1 medium-size onion, coarsely chopped
1 clove garlic, crushed
1/4 cup olive oil
1/2 to 1 teaspoon salt
1/4 teaspoon black pepper
1 cup water
3 medium-size tomatoes, coarsely chopped
1 can sliced and pitted jumbo black olives
Cornstarch, if needed

Put eggplant in salt water and set aside while preparing other ingredients, drain and rinse.

Combine all ingredients, except for tomatoes, olives, and cornstarch, in a large 8-quart stock pot and cook over high heat, covered, for 10 minutes or until desired tenderness. Add tomatoes and olives and cook for another 3 minutes, uncovered.

For a thicker consistency, mix 1/2 to 1 teaspoon cornstarch in cold water, blend thoroughly, and add to pot.

Yellow squash may be added or substituted for variety. This makes an excellent crepe entrée or vegetable side dish.

Yield: 8 to 10 servings.

Bedford Inn

Bill and Betty Ransdell, Innkeepers
561 West Street
Bedford, Kentucky 40006
800-459-4536 (toll free), 502-255-7888
Website: www.bedfordinnky.com

The Bedford Inn is a charming, early American-style country inn on the town square. Bedford is the county seat for rural Trimble County, which borders the Ohio River northeast of Louisville, southwest from Cincinnati, and across from Madison, Indiana.

It is housed in a beautifully restored property thought to have been constructed around 1830, used initially as a tavern. It became the W. F. Peak family residence around 1850 and survived a major fire in 1873. The structure is a two-story brick building of Federal-Greek Revival architecture.

In its present reincarnation, the inn offers overnight lodging in four wonderfully appointed guest rooms, a full and hearty country breakfast in the period decorated dining room, and bargains in the on-site antique and gift shop.

Furnished with antiques and decorated with collectibles throughout, the inn is an attraction in and of itself. Luxurious yet inexpensive, the experience at this inn is a value when compared to nearby alternatives.

Shrimp and Lobster Bisque

2 steamed fresh lobster tails
4 tablespoons butter
1 small white onion, finely chopped
2 stalks celery, finely chopped
2 cloves garlic, minced
1/3 cup all-purpose flour
3 cups chicken broth
1/2 pound steamed medium-size fresh shrimp,
    peeled, deveined, and chopped
2 cups half-and-half
1 (10-ounce) can tomato soup
1 teaspoon cayenne pepper
1/2 teaspoon salt
1/2 teaspoon ground white pepper
1/8 teaspoon fresh nutmeg

Remove lobster meat from shell; coarsely chop and set aside. In a large saucepan, melt butter over medium heat. Add onion, celery, and garlic. Cook for 5 minutes, stirring occasionally. Stir in flour, cook for 2 minutes. Stir in chicken broth, cook for 10 minutes, stirring occasionally until thickened. Add shrimp and lobster meat. Stir in half-and-half, tomato soup, and seasonings. Cook for 10 minutes or until heated through, stirring occasionally. Serve immediately.

Yield: 5 to 6 servings.

Breakfast Crepes

Crepes:

1 1/2 cups evaporated milk
1/3 cup milk
3 eggs
1 egg yolk
3 tablespoons clarified butter
1 1/4 cups flour
1/2 teaspoon salt
Cooked sausage, optional
Mushrooms, optional

Butter Mixture:

4 tablespoons butter
4 tablespoons canola oil

Béchamel Sauce:

4 tablespoons clarified butter
1 tablespoon minced onions or
   1 teaspoon onion powder
6 tablespoons flour
1/8 teaspoon ground thyme
1 teaspoon salt
1/8 teaspoon ground white pepper
1/8 teaspoon ground nutmeg
2 cups milk

To prepare crepes, mix crepe ingredients in a blender until the batter is the consistency of heavy cream. Chill for an hour or two. To prepare butter mixture, melt butter in a 6-inch non-stick fry pan over medium-high heat and add canola oil. Reserve butter mixture for crepes. To make the crepe, preheat a 6-inch nonstick fry pan over medium-high heat. Add a teaspoon of butter mixture to the pan before making each crepe. Pour 1/4 cup of batter into the pan and tilt the pan so that batter covers the entire surface evenly. Cook the crepe for a few minutes, loosen with a spatula, and then turn to cook the other side. Crepes can be made a few days in advance and frozen in stacks of 5 with waxed paper placed between each crepe.

To prepare the béchamel sauce, cook butter in the top of a double broiler until it melts. Sauté onions in butter until translucent. Add flour, thyme, salt, pepper, and nutmeg. Heat milk until it comes to a boil. Add milk to butter mixture and whisk at the same time. A hand blender works well for this task and makes the sauce very creamy. If sauce becomes too thick, add milk. Keep covered.

To serve, coat the inside of the flat crepe with béchamel sauce, add any optional ingredients such as sausage or mushrooms, roll, and pour béchamel sauce over crepes when plated.

Yield: 16 servings (serving size: 2 crepes).

Bennett House

Richard and Rita Smart, Innkeepers
419 West Main Street
Richmond, Kentucky 40475
877-204-3426 (toll free), 859-623-7876
Website: www.bennetthousebb.com

Step through the double oversized entry doors at the Bennett House in Richmond and into the historic Queen Anne Romanesque home. Casual elegance describes the Bennett House, a charming bed and breakfast located in the National Register District near Eastern Kentucky University.

Designed by Samuel E. des Jardins in the late 1800s the two-and-one-half-story asymmetrical brick house boasts stained glass windows and 12-foot high ceilings in spacious rooms. In addition to their comfortable guest rooms and cottage, the home is a beautiful setting for wedding receptions and events. It is open to the public for a tea luncheon on the first Saturday of each month.

Kentucky Sauce for Ice Cream

This recipe goes back to the time of Henry Clay and makes great holiday gifts.

1 cup brown sugar
1 cup white sugar
1 scant cup water
1 orange
1 lemon
1 cup strawberry preserves
1 1/2 cups pecans or walnuts
1 cup bourbon

Cook the first three ingredients in a 3-quart saucepan until it spins a thread. Remove from stove. Grate the rind of the orange and lemon. Cut the orange and lemon into sections. Add strawberry preserves, nuts, whiskey, orange and lemon sections, and rinds. Warm before serving over vanilla or butter pecan ice cream.

Yield: 4 cups (8 to 10 servings).

Apple Casserole

6 to 8 apples, peeled and sliced
1 tablespoon lemon juice
2 tablespoons water
3/4 cup sugar
1/2 cup all-purpose flour
1 1/2 teaspoons cinnamon
1/4 teaspoon salt
1/4 cup butter, chopped
1 cup grated extra sharp Cheddar cheese

Place apples, lemon juice, and water in a 1 1/2-quart glass baking dish. In another bowl, combine sugar, flour, cinnamon, and salt. Sprinkle this topping mixture over the apples. Place butter on the topping mixture and then sprinkle with grated cheese. Bake, uncovered, at 350 degrees for 30 minutes.

This is a great side dish for pork. It creates some good conversation as folks are a little unsure about the combination of cheese, apples, and cinnamon, but they love the taste.

Yield: 6 to 8 servings.

Banana Slush

Prep: 10 to 15 minutes

5 to 6 bananas
3 cups sugar
6 cups water
1 (6-ounce) can frozen lemonade
2 (12-ounce) cans frozen orange juice
1 (46-ounce) can pineapple juice
2 liters ginger ale

Blend bananas in a blender. Combine bananas with sugar, water, and juices. Mix well and pour mixture into three plastic containers. Recipe can be made ahead of time, frozen for 2 or 3 days, before making punch. Let thaw 1 hour before serving. To serve, place large chunks of frozen juice in a punch bowl or pitcher and pour ginger ale gently over the top.

Yield: 50 servings.

The Blue Heron

Connie Hubbard and Liz Huffman, Innkeepers
270 East Prong Road
Richmond, Kentucky 40475
859-527-0186
Website: www.blueheronretreat.com

The Blue Heron, a Victorian-style house patterned after a historic house in Richmond, is situated on a 30-acre farm just minutes from Lexington and Richmond.

This quiet farm setting welcomes individuals and groups for weekend getaways or retreats. Guests may relax on the front porch and deck on sunny days or curl up by the fire on wintry days.

Trails for hiking, benches for resting or reading, plus two waterfalls, which can be seen and heard from the front porch, are ready for discovery.

The inn is a working goat farm and the owners encourage guests to witness the birth of baby goats in the spring and summer.

Crab Dip

1/2 cup chopped onion
1/2 cup chopped celery
1 teaspoon Old Bay seasoning
1 tablespoon margarine or butter
1 pound crab meat
2 (8-ounce) packages cream cheese
1 cup sour cream
4 tablespoons Miracle Whip
3 teaspoons Worcestershire sauce
1/2 teaspoon hot sauce
1/2 teaspoon garlic salt
1/4 cup chopped pecans
1 cup shredded sharp Cheddar cheese, divided

Melt margarine or butter in a skillet over medium-high heat. Add onion, celery, and Old Bay seasoning and sauté until tender. In a large bowl, combine crab meat, cream cheese, sour cream, Miracle Whip, Worcestershire sauce, hot sauce, garlic salt, pecans, and 1/2 cup of the Cheddar cheese. Add the sautéed vegetables to crab meat mixture and place in a 2-quart ovenproof dish. Sprinkle with remaining Cheddar cheese. Bake at 325 degrees for 30 minutes. Serve hot with toast rounds or crackers. This recipe can also be prepared ahead and frozen; thaw and reheat prior to serving.

Yield: 8 to 12 servings.

Chocolate Chip Oatmeal Cake

1 3/4 cups boiling water
1 cup uncooked oatmeal
1 cup brown sugar, lightly packed
1 cup granulated sugar
1 stick margarine or butter
2 extra large eggs
1 3/4 cups unsifted flour
1 teaspoon baking soda
1/2 teaspoon salt
1 tablespoon cocoa
1 (12-ounce) package semisweet chocolate chips, divided
3/4 cup chopped walnuts

Fresh fruit, chocolate sauce, or cream cheese frosting and chocolate chips for garnish

Pour boiling water over oatmeal. Let stand at room temperature for 10 minutes. Add brown sugar, white sugar, and margarine. Stir until margarine melts. Add eggs and mix well. Sift together flour, baking soda, salt, and cocoa. Add flour to sugar mixture and mix well. Add half the package of chocolate chips and stir. Pour batter into a greased and floured 9 x 13-inch pan. Sprinkle walnuts and remaining chocolate chips on top. Bake in a preheated oven at 350 degrees for 40 minutes or until wooden pick comes out clean. This cake may be served several ways; you may garnish with in season fruits, top with chocolate sauce, or ice with cream cheese frosting and sprinkle with chocolate chips.

Yield: 8 to 10 servings.

51

Bluegrass Country Estate
Bed and Breakfast

Cheryl Sabin, Innkeeper
1226 Bluegrass Parkway
LaGrange, Kentucky 40031
877-229-2009 (toll free), 502-222-2009
Website: www.bluegrasscountryestate.com

*B*luegrass Country Estate, a Louisville area bed and breakfast located just outside LaGrange, is a dream come true for Cheryl Sabin, the owner.

Surrounded by horse farms, it offers the perfect getaway, complete with swimming pool, hot tub, full screen theatre room, workout room, and a barn for your horse! It is truly a unique place to stay that promises an unforgettable experience.

Breakfast is served each morning in the formal dining room, in one of the sunrooms, or outside on a private guestroom patio. Surrounded by horse farms, this country estate offers true Kentucky hospitality.

Magic Time Muffins

Prep: 15 minutes

1 stick butter
3/4 cup sugar
2 teaspoons freshly grated lime zest
2 large eggs
5 tablespoons heavy cream
1 cup all-purpose flour
1/4 teaspoon salt
1/2 cup sweetened coconut flakes, divided
1/2 cup blueberries

Beat together the butter, sugar, and zest until light and fluffy. Beat in eggs one at a time. Add the cream, flour, and salt and beat on low until just combined. Stir in the coconut, reserving a small amount to be used later. Fold in blueberries. Spoon batter into muffin cups and sprinkle with remaining coconut. Bake at 350 degrees for 25 to 30 minutes or until edges are golden brown and toothpick comes out clean.

Yield: 8 large or 12 small muffins.

Old Geezer Cake

Prep: 20 minutes

1/3 cup fresh rhubarb,
  chopped into 1/2-inch pieces
2 2/3 cups sugar, divided
2 cups all-purpose flour
1/2 cup vegetable oil
1 egg
1 1/4 cups whole milk, divided
3 tablespoons white vinegar
1 teaspoon baking soda
1 teaspoon cinnamon
1 teaspoon vanilla extract
2 tablespoons butter
1 cup coconut
1 cup chopped pecans

Combine rhubarb pieces and 1/2 cup of the sugar in a small bowl and set aside. In a large mixing bowl, combine all-purpose flour, 1 1/2 cups sugar, vegetable oil, egg, 1 cup milk, vinegar, baking soda, cinnamon, and vanilla extract. Mix together until just combined, add rhubarb and set aside. Pour into a 9 x 13-inch cake pan and bake at 350 degrees for 60 minutes or until a toothpick in the center comes out clean. Set aside to cool.

To make the crunchy topping, combine the butter, coconut, remaining sugar and milk, and pecans. Mix together and cook in a medium saucepan for 3 minutes. Spread topping over the cake while the mixture is still warm.

Yield: 12 servings.

Burlington's Willis Graves
Bed and Breakfast Inn

Nancy and Bob Swartzel, Innkeepers
5825 N. Jefferson Street
Burlington, Kentucky 41005
888-226-5096 (toll free), 859-689-5096
Website: www.burligrave.com

*E*xperience sophisticated charm and relaxed country living at this award-winning inn twenty minutes from Cincinnati. Choose between two masterfully restored early and mid-1800s buildings: the 1830s Federal brick homestead on the National Register Overlay and the 1850s log cabin, both furnished with antiques and reproductions.

In 2006, the inn was chosen to become a Select Registry Distinguished Inns of North America member. Attention to detail is a signature trait with luxurious touches such as whirlpool baths, steam showers, plush robes and towels, fireplaces, fine linens, top quality mattresses, and freshly baked cookies. For comfort and relaxation, enjoy in-room massage, wireless Internet, cable television, DVD players, and a comprehensive movie collection.

Guests experience a full gourmet multiple course breakfast served at individual tables set with white tablecloths, cloth napkins, and fine china. Gracious hospitality and exemplary service abound during your romantic getaway, reunion or business retreat.

Grandmother Wehking's Holland Rusk Custard Dessert

This dessert is a family favorite. The recipe originated with the innkeeper's grandmother, Helen Wehking. It was passed to her mother, Jean Brames, and then to the innkeeper, Nancy Swartzel.

Holland Rusk Toast Crust:

1 (3.5-ounce) package Holland Rusk toast,
  usually found in the cracker aisle
1/2 cup sugar
1/4 pound unsalted butter, melted

Boiled Custard:

1/4 teaspoon salt
1/2 cup sugar
3 teaspoons cornstarch
2 tablespoons all-purpose flour
2 cups cold whole milk
3 egg yolks
1 teaspoon high-quality pure vanilla extract

Meringue:

3 egg whites
3 tablespoons confectioners' sugar

Crush toast to make crumbs. Reserve approximately 1/8 cup of crumbs for the top of dessert. Combine sugar and remaining crumbs in a bowl, add melted butter, and mix thoroughly. Spray a 9-inch springform pan with vegetable spray and line the pan with the crumb mixture.

Mix salt, sugar, cornstarch, and flour together. Add in the milk, followed by the egg yolks and vanilla extract. Heat mixture in the top of a double broiler, stirring frequently until thickened. Remove from stove and let cool. To prevent drying out, place plastic wrap over the top.

Beat egg whites until stiff, add confectioners' sugar, and beat again.

To assemble, pour cooled custard into pan; add meringue and top with reserved bread crumbs. Bake at 200 degrees for 25 minutes until slightly browned. Serve with sweetened whipped cream and fresh raspberries, blackberries, and blueberries.

Yield: 6 to 8 servings.

Crème Brûlée French Toast

Crème Brûlée:

2 cups heavy cream
1/4 cup sugar
Pinch of salt
4 egg yolks
1 teaspoon high-quality pure vanilla extract
Lemon zest, optional

French Toast:

3 average-size, day-old loaves of plain, round French
  or Italian bread
3 eggs
1/2 teaspoon high-quality pure vanilla extract
1/2 cup half-and-half
Butter for griddle
Turbinado sugar (granulated sugar may substitute)
Pure maple syrup

Preheat oven to 300 degrees and have a pot of boiling water ready. In a saucepan over medium heat, combine the cream, sugar, and salt. Cook for 4 to 5 minutes, stirring occasionally until steam rises. In a bowl, beat the egg yolks and vanilla extract until smooth. Pour the hot cream into yolks, a little at a time, stirring constantly, until blended. Divide this mixture among four 6-ounce ramekins. To ensure a smooth consistency, line the bottom of the baking pan or glass dish with a damp kitchen towel before adding the ramekins and boiling water. Place ramekins in the baking pan, add boiling water to fill the pan halfway up the sides of ramekins. Cover loosely with aluminum foil and bake until custard is set, 25 to 30 minutes. Chill for 2 to 3 hours.

Cut bread into 1 3/4-inch thick slices. Using a serrated knife, cut a deep pocket on the side of each slice but do not cut all the way through. Fill each pocket with as much crème brûlée as possible; typically 1 1/2 to 2 tablespoons. The French toast can be prepared in advance and placed in the freezer at this stage. When ready to use, take slices out of the freezer, defrost in the microwave, and proceed.

In a shallow dish, whisk together eggs, vanilla extract, and half-and-half. Place filled bread pieces in the egg mixture and let stand until the bread is saturated, turning bread to coat all sides.

To prepare, melt approximately 3 tablespoons of butter in a large skillet or griddle for each serving. Add bread and cook until toast is golden brown on all sides and the filling is hot. Sprinkle sugar lightly on top of hot bread and use a kitchen torch to caramelize sugar, using small circular motions just above the surface. Be careful not to use too much sugar on top of the bread, or it will be too hard to eat. Serve immediately with a side of pure maple syrup. Add fresh fruit or a serving of bacon or sausage to this delicious treat!

Yield: 10 to 15 servings (serving size: 2 to 3 pieces).

Shrimp and Grits

This savory dish was created by Kristy Charles-Gertz, the former owner of a local restaurant. Kristy's attention to subtle flavor details is obvious in this signature recipe. She has graciously shared her recipes with our inn.

Shrimp Marinade:

1/2 teaspoon fennel seeds for toasting
1/2 teaspoon black peppercorns for toasting
1/4 teaspoon red pepper flakes
1 tablespoon Worcestershire sauce
4 tablespoons extra-virgin olive oil
1 tablespoon sorghum
1/4 cup bourbon
3 cloves garlic, minced
1 bay leaf
1/2 teaspoon lemon zest
1 1/2 pounds large fresh shrimp,
    peeled and deveined with tails on

White Cheddar Grits Cake:

1 quart unsalted chicken stock
1/2 teaspoon kosher salt
2 teaspoons minced fresh garlic
1 cup Weisenberger stone-ground
    yellow grits
2 large eggs, at room temperature
4 egg yolks, at room temperature
1 cup grated sharp white Cheddar cheese
    (4 year English is best)
1 teaspoon baking powder
Dash of hot sauce
Salt to taste
Pepper to taste
Unsalted butter for coating

Sauce for Shrimp and Grits:

2 tablespoons butter
24 marinated shrimp,
    peeled and deveined, with tails on
2 tablespoons shallots
1 clove garlic, minced
1 cup sliced shiitake mushrooms
2 tablespoons shrimp marinade, divided
1/4 cup bourbon
1/2 cup chicken stock
1/2 cup heavy cream
1 tablespoon fresh thyme
1/4 cup applewood-smoked bacon,
    cooked and chopped
2 tablespoons fresh chives
3/4 cup cherry or grape tomatoes,
    sliced in half lengthwise
Salt to taste
Pepper to taste
Shaved Parmesan for garnish to taste

To prepare marinade, lightly toast fennel seeds and black peppercorns in a small, dry sauté pan on medium heat, taking care not to burn. Remove from pan when they start to become aromatic. When cool, grind the fennel seeds, black peppercorns, and red pepper flakes together. Mixture can be stored in an airtight container for days.

In a non-reactive container (glass or stainless steel), combine the remaining marinade ingredients except the shrimp. Stir well. You can refrigerate marinade for three days ahead but do not add the toasted season mix until you are ready to marinate the shrimp. When ready, add shrimp to the marinade and toss occasionally, making sure to coat all parts of shrimp. Marinate for 30 minutes. Never ever re-use marinade!

To prepare grit cakes, grease an 8 x 11-inch baking pan with unsalted butter. In a saucepan over high heat, bring stock to a boil. Slowly stir in salt, garlic, and grits. Reduce heat to medium, cook stirring frequently, until grits have the thickened. Set aside and let cool. Use a mixer to whisk eggs and yolks, whisk until double in size. Whisk the eggs into the grits until mixed. Add the cheese, baking powder, hot sauce, and salt and pepper. Pour grits into the buttered pan and bake at 350 degrees for 20 to 30 minutes. Cool and then refrigerate. Grit cakes can be made 2 to 3 days ahead. Cut into desired shape and reheat in oven to serve.

To prepare sauce, melt butter in 12-inch sauté pan over medium heat; add shrimp and sauté 2 to 3 minutes. Remove shrimp and hold on a room temperature plate. Add shallots and garlic. Cook for about 2 minutes on medium heat. Add mushrooms and cook until limp. Add 1 tablespoon of marinade and add bourbon and flame over medium heat. Add stock and shrimp. Cook shrimp about 2 to 3 minutes or until pink. Add heavy cream, working very quickly. Add thyme, bacon, chives, tomatoes, and season with salt and pepper. Remove shrimp to plate around grit cake. Reduce sauce if needed, it should lightly coat a spoon. Nape sauce around the shrimp. Sprinkle with remaining bacon and shaved Parmesan.

Yield: 6 servings.

Willis Graves' Shiitake Mushroom Soup

2 1/2 cups thinly sliced mushrooms,
  shiitake are our favorite
1/4 cup diced onion
4 cups chicken stock
1 cup beef stock
4 tablespoons butter
1/4 cup all-purpose flour
1 cup half-and-half
Salt to taste
Pepper to taste
1/4 cup white wine (sweeter is better),
  apple juice can substitute
  if you do not want to use wine

Place the mushrooms and onion in a stock pot with the chicken and beef stock; simmer for about 20 minutes until tender. Melt the butter in a separate pan. Work the flour and butter together to make a paste and then whisk into the soup very slowly. Stir in the half-and-half and season with salt and pepper. Add the wine and serve.

Sometimes we add about 1 cup of chopped, cooked chicken breast. We think a glass of apple juice is a good companion while enjoying the soup.

Yield: 4 servings.

60

The Dirty Pig Martini

While owning a restaurant in Burlington, Kristy Charles-Gertz created this signature martini. Kristy describes The Dirty Pig martini as a mini meal; it reflects her creative abilities in the kitchen.

1/2 cup peanut oil
4 slices Kentucky country ham,
** thinly sliced**
12 ounces Grey Goose vodka
2 ounces olive brine
** (juice from olive jar; buy good quality**
** large green olives)**
8 to 12 bleu cheese stuffed olives
Dash of freshly cracked black pepper

Heat oil in a heavy skillet over medium heat. Gently place the ham flat into the hot oil and cover with a mesh screen; the salt in the ham may cause the oil to splatter. Fry the ham until golden brown and place on a paper towel to cool. The ham can be made ahead.

For each martini, combine 6 parts (3-ounces) vodka and 1 part (1/2-ounce) olive brine with cracked ice in a cocktail shaker and shake well. Strain into a chilled martini glass and garnish with ham slices and several bleu cheese olives. Finish with cracked black pepper.

Yield: 4 martinis.

Willis Graves' Three Cheese Tart

1/2 cup sliced mushrooms
1/2 cup sliced tomatoes
1 (9-inch) homemade or high-quality,
  store-bought pie crust
Salt to taste
Pepper to taste
2/3 cup crumbled feta cheese
1 3/4 cups grated Parmesan cheese
8-ounces grated Gruyère cheese
4 eggs
3/4 cup heavy cream
1/4 cup white wine
Ground cayenne red pepper
  for a little kick
Extra grated Parmesan
  to sprinkle on top of tart
Freshly cracked black pepper

Bake empty pie crust at 350 degrees for 12 minutes, remove from oven and let cool for approximately 10 minutes before adding other ingredients.

Once the pie crust is cool, place mushrooms and tomatoes in the bottom of the pie crust and season with salt and pepper. Add all of the cheeses on top of the mushrooms and tomatoes.

In a separate bowl, mix eggs, heavy cream, white wine, and cayenne pepper to taste. Be careful with the cayenne pepper.

Slowly pour egg mixture over pie and sprinkle extra Parmesan cheese and freshly cracked pepper on top.

Bake at 350 degrees for 1 hour.

Yield: 6 to 8 servings.

Central Park Bed and Breakfast

Nancy and Kevin Hopper, Innkeepers
1353 South Fourth Street
Louisville, Kentucky 40208
800-638-1505, 502-638-1505
Website: www.centralparkbandb.com

More than a simple inn or hotel, Central Park Bed and Breakfast offers relaxing lodging accommodations, delightful breakfasts, complimentary beverages and snacks, and a romantic atmosphere.

Conveniently located in the heart of historic Old Louisville, the inn is just a few blocks off Interstate 65 and only minutes from Louisville International Airport.

Listed on the National Historic Register and a member of Select Registry Distinguished Inns of North America, this magnificent three-story residence, constructed in 1884, displays an ambiance of fine period furnishings and examples of exquisite hand craftsmanship. The historic neighborhood features America's largest collection of Victorian homes, and is a wonderful step back in time.

The inn has a total of 18 rooms with 12 fireplaces. The seven guestrooms are decorated with period antiques and furnishings, yet contain many modern comforts. Breakfast is served fireside in the formal dining room.

With Central Park located across the street, this area offers opportunities for rest or recreation with ample space for walking, jogging, playing tennis, or just watching the world go by.

Orange Slices in Lime Syrup

Prep: 15 minutes

4 oranges
1/2 cup dry white wine
1/2 cup sugar
1 1/2 teaspoons anise seeds
1 lime grated for zest
1 lime, juiced
Flower or mint leaf, optional for garnish

Peel oranges, removing as much bitter white pith as possible. Using a cutting board that catches juice, slice oranges into 1/2-inch thick rounds. Place in an appropriate sized bowl with the orange juice.

In a medium saucepan, mix the wine, sugar, and anise seeds. Bring to boil over high heat. Reduce heat to medium, cooking until liquid reduces to 1/2 cup, approximately 25 to 30 minutes.

Strain the syrup. Stir in the lime juice and zest. Refrigerate at least 1 hour or overnight. Serve in shallow bowls or dishes, garnished with a flower or mint leaf.

Yield: 4 servings.

Lemon Tea Bread and Raspberry Butter

Bread:

1/2 cup butter, at room temperature
1 1/4 cups sugar, divided
2 large eggs
1/2 cup milk
1 1/2 cups all-purpose flour
1 teaspoon baking powder
1/2 teaspoon salt
Zest and juice from 1 lemon

Raspberry Butter:

1/2 cup butter, softened
2 tablespoons dry milk powder, divided
1/2 cup seedless raspberry jam
1/2 cup confectioners' sugar

In a large bowl, cream butter and 1 cup of the sugar. Beat in eggs and milk. Stir in flour, baking powder, and salt. Pour into greased mini-loaf pans. Bake at 350 degrees for 30 to 40 minutes. Mix the remaining 1/4 cup sugar with the lemon juice and zest. Spoon over the mini-loaves while they are still warm. Serve with Raspberry Butter.

To prepare raspberry butter, process the butter until smooth in a food processor. Scrape down as necessary. Add 1 tablespoon powdered milk, jam, and sugar. Add the remaining powdered milk and process until smooth, scraping as necessary. Store refrigerated in a sealed container. Serve with Lemon Tea Bread.

Yield: 8 servings.

Christopher's Bed and Breakfast

Brenda Guidugli, Owner and Innkeeper
604 Poplar Street
Bellevue, Kentucky 41073
888-585-7085 (toll free), 859-491-9354
Website: www.christophersbb.com

Located near Northern Kentucky's bustling Newport on the Levee, Christopher's is a ravishing 19th century former church that sparkles with jewel-toned stained-glass windows, three sumptuous Jacuzzi suites, and sits grandly in the heart of Bellevue. The City of Bellevue was recently awarded "One of the Top 10 Neighborhoods to Live" by *Cincinnati Magazine*.

Named after St. Christopher, the Patron Saint of Travelers, this unique inn is the former home of the Bellevue Christian Church. Christopher's sits in one of the area's three historic districts, Taylor's Daughters, in honor of General James Taylor. The spacious building, decorated and furnished in a Victorian style, features the original hardwood floors and stained-glass windows.

Christopher's has been written up in regional and national magazines and voted by inngoers for three consecutive years in *Arrington's Bed and Breakfast Journal's Book of Lists* as "one of the top 15 B&Bs/Inns for Best Design and Décor."

Best Egg Casserole Ever

Prep: 15 minutes

12 eggs
1 cup plain yogurt
1 teaspoon seasoned salt, or to taste
6 tablespoons (3/4 stick) butter or margarine
1/4 cup (or less) chopped onion
2 cups shredded hash brown potatoes, thawed
1 cup grated sharp Cheddar cheese

Beat eggs, yogurt, and salt together. Melt butter in a large pan, slightly sauté onion and stir in potatoes. Pour the egg mixture into potato mixture and lightly stir to blend ingredients. Pour into a greased 2-quart casserole. Sprinkle with grated cheese.

Bake at 350 degrees for approximately 25 minutes or until a knife inserted into center comes out clean.

Yield: 8 servings.

Country Charm Historic Farmhouse
Bed and Breakfast

David and LaVonna Snell, Innkeepers
505 Hutchison Road
Paris, Kentucky 40361
866-988-1006 (toll free), 859-988-1006
Website: www.countrycharm.net

Francis Hall, whose father emigrated from Yorkshire, England, built the triple-brick thick Gothic Revival house in 1869. In 1945, David Snell's grandfather, Harold W. Snell, purchased 300 acres from the Ritter family of RIT dyes fame. A year later, David's family moved to the historic Hall farmhouse.

Country Charm Historic Farmhouse Bed and Breakfast sits atop a hill overlooking 65 acres of Kentucky farmland. Located off a beautiful four-lane highway between Lexington and Paris, it offers a serene, relaxed rural atmosphere.

Baked Oatmeal

Prep: 5 minutes

1/2 cup unsweetened applesauce
3/4 cup brown sugar
1/2 cup egg substitute
1 teaspoon salt
3 cups uncooked quick-cooking oats
1 teaspoon cinnamon
2 teaspoons baking powder
1 cup fat-free milk

Mix all ingredients together and pour into a greased 8 x 8-inch square pan. Bake at 350 degrees for 30 minutes. Serve with fruit, maple syrup, sugar, or warm milk.

Yield: 6 to 8 servings.

The Doctor's Inn

Bill and Biji Baker, Innkeepers
617 Chestnut Street
Berea, Kentucky 40403
859-986-3042
Website: www.berea.com/docsinn

Grilled Leg of Lamb

Lamb:

**Whole leg of lamb (college age),
ask the butcher to bone and flatten**
1/2 cup fresh mint
1/2 cup mustard
1 small onion, grated
Freshly ground pepper

Sauce:

1/4 pound butter, divided
1/2 clove garlic
1 tablespoon grated onion
1/2 cup chopped fresh mint
Salt to taste
Pepper to taste

To prepare lamb, 2 hours before cooking, make small shallow slashes all over the meat and insert little pieces of fresh mint. Rub the lamb with mustard, grated onion, and ground pepper. Let stand while preparing the sauce.

To prepare sauce, melt approximately 1 tablespoon of butter in a small heavy pan. Add the garlic and onion and cook gently for a few minutes. Remove and discard the garlic. Add the chopped mint and the remaining butter until well combined. The sauce will be used for basting.

When the fire is ready, place the lamb on a metal grill. Baste constantly with the sauce while cooking. Salt and pepper the roast halfway through cooking. The meat should be ready in 30 to 45 minutes, depending on the heat of the fire. Boil the remaining sauce and serve over the lamb.

Yield: 8 to 10 servings.

For gracious Kentucky hospitality, the Doctor's Inn is Berea's premier bed and breakfast. Nestled in the foothills of the Appalachians just off Interstate 75 in the heart of Kentucky's designated capital of Folk Arts and Crafts, the inn offers elegant lodging and a warm welcome.

This Greek Revival home was built by Bill's father and mother, Dr. John Baker and Mattye Belle Kincaid. After years away from Berea, Bill and his wife, Biji, returned to his hometown to fulfill their dreams.

Guestrooms are appointed with genuine Berea College antique furniture, oriental rugs, and stained glass windows. The inn boasts a baby grand piano, plus a library of books and magazines. Enjoy a game of golf nearby or stroll the Berea College campus and watch the students work at their many industries. Breathtaking views, comfort, and hospitality await guests.

Christmas Wassail

1 pound sugar
1 quart water or cranberry juice
2 whole cloves
3 sticks cinnamon
4 allspice berries or
  1 teaspoon ground allspice
1 1/2 tablespoons ground ginger
3 cups orange juice
1 1/2 cups lemon juice
2 quarts apple juice

Combine sugar and water in a saucepan or slow cooker. Add spices, cover, and let stand on low heat for 1 hour. Add orange, lemon, and apple juices and reheat. Remove spices to serve. Serves best after heating or refrigerate and reheat as needed.

Yield: 16 to 20 servings
(serving size: 1 mug).

Chili Con Carne Authentique

Prep: 20 minutes

1 cup chopped onion
2 tablespoons oil
1 1/2 pounds ground beef
1 garlic clove, minced
1 tablespoon salt
2 cups tomato sauce
2 cups whole tomatoes
1 cup water
3 tablespoons chili powder
1 tablespoon ground cumin
1/4 teaspoon hot sauce
1/4 teaspoon black pepper
1/4 ounce unsweetened
  baking chocolate
1/4 cup sherry, optional
1 to 3 (16-ounce) cans
  red kidney beans, optional

Sauté the onion in oil until translucent and tender. Add the beef, garlic, and salt. Cook, stirring until meat is browned. Add tomato sauce, tomatoes, water, chili powder, cumin, hot sauce, black pepper, and chocolate. Cover and simmer 2 1/2 hours, adding more water as necessary, stirring frequently. Add sherry in the last thirty minutes of cooking. Add up to 3 cans of red kidney beans, if desired. Serve over rice, spaghetti or noodles.

Yield: 4 to 6 servings.

DuPont Mansion

Gayle and Herbert Warren, Owners
1317 South Fourth Street
Louisville, Kentucky 40208
(502) 638-0045
Website: www.dupontmansion.com

The magnificent DuPont Mansion stands proudly along Fourth Street in historic Old Louisville. The entire neighborhood is a national treasure and is experiencing an exciting renaissance as depicted in the 2007 release of the PBS film documentary *Mansions of Old Louisville.* The opening scene of this film features the front parlor of the DuPont Mansion.

Once the home of wealthy industrialists, the DuPont Mansion today stands open to those seeking a place of comfort and peace, just blocks away from the University of Louisville and Churchill Downs to the south and Louisville's thriving downtown and riverfront to the north.

A proud recipient of the Louisville Historic League's 2002 award for historic renovation, the DuPont Mansion is the perfect venue for overnight, weekend, or extended stays.

Champagne Punch

12 lemons, juiced
Confectioners' sugar to taste
1 quart carbonated water
Block of ice for serving
1/2 pint curaçao
1 pint brandy
2 quarts champagne

To prepare, sweeten the lemon juice to taste with confectioners' sugar. Add carbonated water. Place a large block of ice in a punch bowl and add juice mixture. Stir well. Add remaining ingredients. Stir. Decorate with in season fruits. Serve in 4-ounce punch glasses.

Yield: 35 servings.

Banana Toffee Pie

Graham Cracker Crust:

1 1/2 cups graham cracker crumbs
1/2 cup turbinado sugar
1 stick butter, melted
3 teaspoons ground ginger

Filling:

1 (14-ounce) can sweetened condensed
  milk, do not use evaporated milk
2 bananas, sliced
2 cups whipping cream

To prepare crust, mix graham cracker crumbs, sugar, melted butter, and ginger until well blended. Press mixture into a 9-inch pie plate and cool in the refrigerator.

Remove label from the can of sweetened condensed milk; do not use evaporated milk. Place the unopened can in the bottom of a deep pot, such as a Dutch oven, and cover with water so that water is above the top of the can. Boil the unopened can in water for 3 hours. Monitor closely to make sure there is always enough water in the pan. Remove can from the heat and let cool 10 to 15 minutes.

To prepare the pie, open the can and pour toffee into piecrust. Allow to cool. Slice the bananas over the toffee. Whip the whipping cream until peaks form and spoon on top of bananas. Refrigerate before serving.

Yield: 8 servings.

Corn Chowder

Prep: 25 minutes

1/2 pound sliced bacon
1/2 cup chopped onion
1 cup chopped celery
2 tablespoons all-purpose flour
4 cups whole milk
1/8 teaspoon black pepper
1 (14.75-ounce) can cream-style corn
1 (15-ounce) can tiny whole potatoes,
    drained and diced or fresh diced potatoes
Fresh chopped parsley or green onions,
    optional
Paprika to taste, optional

In a large saucepan, cook bacon over medium heat for 8 to 10 minutes, stirring occasionally, or until fully cooked and crisp. Drain fat, reserving 3 tablespoons in saucepan. Drain bacon on paper towels and set aside.

Cook onion, celery, and flour in bacon fat over medium heat for 5 minutes, stirring constantly, until mixture is bubbly and then remove from heat. Gradually stir in milk. Reheat and bring to a boil, stirring constantly for 1 minute. Stir in black pepper, corn, potatoes and bacon.

To serve, sprinkle each serving with parsley or green onions and a dash of paprika.

Yield: 6 servings.

Farm House Inn

Peg Taylor, Innkeeper
735 Taylor Branch Road
Parkers Lake, Kentucky 42634
606-376-7383
Website: www.farmhouseinnbb.com

The Farm House Inn, once home to generations of farm families, is surrounded by historic farmland and the Daniel Boone National Forest in southern Kentucky. It offers comfortable bedrooms in a 1920s log house and welcomes 21st century families with children who may gather eggs from the chickens who supply fresh eggs for breakfast. The farm's dogs often serve as tour guides, leading visitors to cliffs that once sheltered native American families and hunters.

The Inn is located between Cumberland Falls and the Big South Fork National River and Recreation Area. A nature lover's paradise, the spectacular cliff lines, fishing ponds, and wild life areas make interesting destinations for photographers, nature lovers, and those who need to walk off the innkeeper's generous breakfasts.

Farm House Inn Shirred Eggs

Prep: 10 minutes

1 slice breakfast ham
Small handful shredded Cheddar,
   Monterey Jack, Colby or Mexican cheese
1 free range or organic egg
3 tablespoons half-and-half
Freshly ground pepper (black, white, or red) to taste
Red pepper flakes to taste
Dried seasonings (basil, rosemary, or tarragon)
Fresh parsley to taste
1 toasted English muffin

Spray an individual baking dish with butter-flavor cooking spray. Place ham on bottom of the dish and put a small handful of shredded cheese on top, making a nest for the egg. Break the fresh egg into the well in the middle of the cheese, and pour the half-and-half over the top of the egg. Sprinkle a scant handful of cheese, pepper, parsley, red pepper flakes, and dreid seasonings over the top of the egg.

Bake at 375 degrees for 20 minutes or until golden and whites are set. When baking is complete, snip fresh parsley over top. Serve immediately, while hot and bubbly, on a toasted English muffin or favorite piece of toasted bread.

Yield: 1 serving.

Breakfast Oats Parfaits

1 cup quick-cooking or old-fashioned oats,
  uncooked
2 (8-ounce) cartons nonfat or vanilla yogurt
1 (8-ounce) can crushed pineapple in juice,
  undrained
2 tablespoons sliced almonds
2 cups sliced fresh or frozen strawberries
Whipped cream, optional

In a medium bowl, combine oats, yogurt, pineapple, and almonds. Mix well, cover and refrigerate overnight. To serve, layer oat mixture and strawberries in 4 parfait glasses. Garnish with additional strawberries and add a little whipped cream if desired.

Yield: 4 servings.

Federal Grove Bed and Breakfast

Lanny and Terry Harlow, Innkeepers
475 East Main Street
Auburn, Kentucky 42206
270-542-6106
Website: www.bbonline.com/ky/fedgrove/index.html

This Federal-style home was built circa 1871 in Logan County and sits on land that was a Federal Land Grant given to Jonathan Clark, brother of William Clark, of the famous Lewis and Clark Expedition. Today, Federal Grove Bed and Breakfast is one of almost 100 homes listed on the National Register of Historical Homes in the lovely town of Auburn.

Cherry, walnut, and oak antique furniture occupy Federal Grove's elegant rooms. Guests will enjoy the inn's selection of antiques which are for sale, and the many Auburn antique shops.

The Shaker Museum and the National Corvette Museum in Bowling Green are only a few miles away.

Federal Grove Skillet Omelet

1/4 cup olive oil
3 eggs
3 tablespoons sour cream
1 tablespoon chopped onion
1 tablespoon chopped green pepper
1 tablespoon chopped red pepper
Salt to taste
Pepper to taste
1/2 cup shredded sharp Cheddar or
  Colby cheese, divided
1/8 cup fresh tomatoes for garnish
Chopped parsley or basil for garnish

Heat a 6-inch cast-iron skillet over medium heat and then add olive oil. In a separate bowl, whisk together the eggs and sour cream. Pour mixture into the heated skillet. Add the onion, green pepper, red pepper, salt, and pepper. Stir eggs as they start to cook and then add 1/4 cup shredded cheese. Do not stir too much, but stir occasionally so that egg does not stick to the pan.

Turn the skillet off and sprinkle with the remaining cheese. Place a lid on the skillet and let sit for about 5 minutes. Eggs should be very easy to remove from skillet if pan is seasoned. To serve, garnish with fresh tomatoes and sprinkle herbs over top of eggs.

Yield: 1 serving.

Sweet and Sour Muffins

Prep: 10 minutes

2 sticks butter
1 cup sugar
1 cup sour cream
2 cups self-rising flour, divided

Cream butter and sugar together. Add sour cream and mix well. Slowly add in flour, mixing after each 1/2 cup. Spoon batter into small ungreased muffin tins. Bake at 350 degrees for 20 to 30 minutes.

Yield: 12 muffins.

House on Belmont

Lora and Peter Hessing, Innkeepers
331 Belmont Avenue
Winchester, Kentucky 40391
859-744-4485
Website: www.houseonbelmont.com

The House on Belmont has three lovely guestrooms set in the historic Dr. Johnson House, built in 1872. The house has been extensively renovated with modern conveniences. In addition to hosting overnight guests, special event teas may be reserved in advance for small groups.

Winchester, with its quaint downtown, is situated just 20 minutes southeast of Lexington with quick access to the city without a "big city hassle." Charming antique and gift shops dot Main Street, and the town is home to the Bluegrass Museum.

Quiche Lora's Style

Prep: 15 minutes

8 ounces Gruyère or
  4 ounces of Monterey Jack cheese, grated
1 (9-inch) pie crust
6 eggs
1 cup half-and-half
2 teaspoons nutmeg
1 teaspoon cinnamon
1/2 teaspoon salt

For Quiche Lorraine, add:

4 ounces (4 to 5 slices) crispy bacon, crumbled
8 ounces diced ham
2 tablespoons chopped green onion

For Veggie Quiche, add:

1 cup chopped fresh mushrooms
1 cup chopped broccoli
1/2 cup chopped green onion
1 cup chopped red and green pepper

Alternately layer cheese and other chosen fillings into pie crust. Combine eggs, half-and-half, and spices in blender just until mixed. Pour this mixture over cheese and meat or veggies. Recipe can also be divided by four and baked in 10-ounce custard cups for individual servings.

Bake at 375 degrees for approximately 30 minutes, until top is lightly browned.

Yield: 8 servings.

Tiramisu Parfaits

Prep: 20 minutes, overnight chilling

1/2 cup coffee liqueur
1/2 cup water
1/4 cup dark corn syrup
2 tablespoons instant espresso powder or
  coffee powder
2 tablespoons plus 3/4 cup confectioners' sugar,
  divided
1 (8-ounce) package cream cheese,
  at room temperature
2 ounces quality dark chocolate
1 1/2 cups whipping cream, chilled
1 (12-ounce) purchased pound cake,
  cut into 12 slices

Combine coffee liqueur, water, dark corn syrup, espresso powder, and 2 tablespoons confectioners' sugar in small saucepan. Bring slowly to a boil and stir until well blended. Allow to cool to room temperature.

Combine 5 tablespoons of coffee mixture, 1/2 cup confectioners' sugar, and cream cheese in a large mixer bowl. Using a mixer, beat until smooth and fluffy. In a food processor, process chocolate until finely chopped. Add to cream cheese mixture.

Beat whipping cream and 1/4 cup confectioners' sugar until stiff peaks form. Fold whipped cream into cream cheese mixture. Slice pound cake slices into 3 strips each and put 1 slice into each of 6 parfait glasses. Drizzle 1 tablespoon espresso syrup mixture over each. Spread 1/3 cup of cream cheese filling over each. Repeat layers of cake, syrup, and cream cheese filling. Cover and refrigerate 6 hours or overnight. Top with reserved dark chocolate.

Yield: 6 servings.

Lyndon House Bed and Breakfast

Terry Anton Giovanetto, Innkeeper
507 North Broadway
Lexington, Kentucky 40508
800-494-9597 (toll free), 859-225-3631
Website: www.lyndonhouse.com

Raspberry-Apple Relish

Prep: 20 minutes, chill overnight

1 navel orange
1 (12-ounce) bag frozen raspberries
2 large Granny Smith apples, peeled and grated
2 cups sugar

Grate the orange peel and set aside. Peel the skin from the orange and discard. Cut the orange into four pieces and set aside. Place 1/2 of the raspberries and two sections of the orange in a food processor and mix to an even consistency. Spoon the mixture into a bowl. Repeat this step. Stir the apples, grated orange peels, and sugar into the bowl. Cover and refrigerate for at least 4 hours or overnight.

This relish is a nice complement to French toast or sweet breakfast breads when served on the side. It will keep for one week in the refrigerator in an airtight container. It may also be frozen for longer storage.

Yield: 12 to 16 servings.

*L*ocated in Lexington's charming downtown, this historic house is well-appointed with stylish furnishings and all the comforts of a home-like atmosphere. Each guest room is spacious with 11-foot ceilings, trimmed with elegant moldings, comfortable bedding, over stuffed chairs, and complete with a full bath. Each morning guests awaken to the aroma of fresh coffee and are treated to a delicious breakfast prepared by the innkeeper.

Some of the city's finest restaurants and shops, as well as the downtown nightlife, are within walking distance. After a day of sightseeing, the beautiful garden is an ideal backdrop for a relaxing retreat. The Lyndon House is the perfect environment for discussing the day's events with other guests or curling up with a book in a cozy corner.

Baked Chicken Marsala

Marsala:

1/2 cup dry bread crumbs
1/2 cup grated Parmesan cheese
1/4 cup chopped fresh cilantro
1/2 teaspoon paprika
Salt to taste
Pepper to taste
8 boneless chicken breasts,
  pounded and halved
1/4 cup butter, melted
1/2 cup marsala wine

Mushroom Sauce:

1/4 cup butter
1 pound sliced mushrooms
1/2 cup marsala wine

To prepare chicken, coat a 9 x 13-inch baking dish with a nonstick cooking spray. Combine the first 6 ingredients to make a dry mix. Dip the chicken in the dry mix, coat on both sides, and place the chicken in the baking dish (overlapping the chicken in 2 rows). Drizzle melted butter over the chicken and bake covered for 30 minutes. Add the marsala wine and bake, covered, for 15 minutes. Uncover and bake at 350 degrees for an additional 10 minutes.

To prepare the mushroom sauce, melt the butter with some of the chicken drippings (2 teaspoons or to taste) in a saucepan over medium heat. Add the mushrooms and sauté for 1 minute. Add the marsala wine and continue simmering for another 2 to 3 minutes, until it begins to thicken. Arrange the chicken on a platter, pour the sauce over the chicken and serve.

Yield: 8 to 12 servings.

Market Street Inn

Carol and Steve Stenbro, Innkeepers
330 West Market Street
Jeffersonville, Indiana 47130
888-284-1877 (toll free), 812-285-1877
Website: www.innonmarket.com

Welcome to Market Street Inn, a stately Second Empire 1881 mansion in downtown Jeffersonville, Indiana, just across the river from Louisville. It is only two blocks from restaurants and a historic shopping district and one block from the Ohio River.

The entire mansion has 10,000+ square feet, with seven beautiful guest rooms, including three large suites. Before becoming a bed and breakfast, it was nearly destroyed by two devastating fires in 1996 but fully restored in 2005.

The inn's charming two dining rooms can accommodate up to 32 people with food prepared by a professional chef. A large, third floor deck with fountain and outside fireplace are additional amenities.

Market Street Bran Muffins

Prep: 15 minutes

4 cups All-Bran cereal
2 cups Bran Flakes cereal
1 teaspoon salt
2 cups boiling water
1 quart buttermilk
2 cups sugar
1 cup shortening or vegetable oil
4 eggs, slightly beaten
5 cups all-purpose flour
5 teaspoons baking soda

Combine first 5 ingredients and let sit for 5 minutes.

Cream sugar and shortening, or vegetable oil, until smooth. Add beaten eggs and mix until well blended. Sift flour and baking soda and gradually add to egg mixture until well blended. Add to the All-Bran mixture and combine thoroughly.

Store batter in a covered bowl or container in the refrigerator. To bake, fill cups for a full, puffy muffin. For variation, you may also add raisins, nuts, and/or pineapple. Bake in greased muffin tins at 325 degrees for 20 to 25 minutes. Batter will keep up to six weeks in the refrigerator, but do not stir.

Yield: 6 dozen.

Tomato Bisque

1 (15-ounce) can diced tomatoes
1 (15-ounce) can diced tomatoes with green chiles
2 (10-ounce) cans condensed tomato soup, undiluted
1 1/2 cups milk
1 teaspoon sugar
1 teaspoon dried basil
1 teaspoon paprika
1/4 teaspoon garlic powder
1 (8-ounce) container sour cream

In a medium saucepan, combine all of the ingredients except the sour cream. You can substitute 2 cans of stewed tomatoes for the two varieties of diced tomatoes. Bring to a boil. Reduce heat, cover, and simmer 10 minutes. Stir in sour cream until blended and serve.

Yield: 8 servings (serving size: 1 cup).

Chocolate Waffles

Prep: 15 minutes

3 eggs
2 cups milk
3 cups Bisquick flour
6 tablespoons (3/4 stick) melted butter
1 1/2 ounces unsweetened chocolate, melted
2 1/2 ounces semisweet chocolate, melted
1 quart fresh strawberries, sliced and sweetened to taste
1/2 pint whipping cream

Whisk eggs and milk in a large mixing bowl. Gradually add flour and beat until smooth. Add melted butter to the flour mixture. Fold in melted chocolate and stir until blended thoroughly. Ladle 1/2 cup of mixture onto waffle iron and bake for 3 to 4 minutes. Remove waffle from waffle iron and place on serving plate. Top with strawberries and a dollop of whipping cream.

Yield: 6 waffles.

Meek House

Sara and Jim Call, Innkeepers
119 East Third Street
Frankfort, Kentucky 40601
866-646-7650 (toll free), 502-227-2566
Website: www.bbonline.com/ky/meek

*T*his charming Gothic Revival home takes its name from the man who built it in 1869, Benjamin J. Meek, a silversmith who helped develop the Meek and Milam fishing reel. The inn's spacious rooms and quiet surroundings make it a pleasant retreat.

Its location, a half block east of Capital Avenue and Third Street, is within walking distance of the Kentucky State Capitol and historic downtown Frankfort's many attractions.

Baked Eggs with Herbs and Cheese

This recipe was adapted from *How to Start and Operate Your Own Bed and Breakfast* by Martha Watson Murphy. We serve this to most of our guests on their first morning with us.

1/2 tablespoon melted butter
1 egg
1 tablespoon half-and-half
1 tablespoon grated white Cheddar or sharp Cheddar cheese
Pinch of herbes de Provence or other Italian herbs or
   fresh herbs
Parmesan cheese, grated
Black pepper to taste
English muffin half

Pour melted butter into an individual serving size ramekin or custard dish. Break the egg into the dish. Pour in half-and-half and then sprinkle grated Cheddar cheese over the half-and-half. Sprinkle herbes de Provence, a dusting of Parmesan cheese, and a little ground black pepper over top. Place ramekin in a baking dish; carefully add water until the ramekin is sitting in about 1/2-inch of water. Bake at 350 degrees for 20 minutes.

To serve, run a knife or rubber spatula around the edge of the ramekin, drain off any excess liquid, and slip the baked egg onto a toasted English muffin half. Serve immediately.

Variation: The baked egg may be served on a muffin topped with Canadian bacon, a thick slice of tomato, or 2 pieces of crisp bacon.

Yield: 1 serving.

Myrtledene Bed and Breakfast

James Spragens, Innkeeper
370 North Spalding Avenue
Lebanon, Kentucky 40033
800-391-1721 (toll free), 270-692-2223
Website: www.myrtledene.com

Myrtledene was built in 1833 by the founder of Lebanon, Benedict Spalding, who was a prominent local businessman and state representative.

During the Civil War, Spalding and his home were the unwilling hosts to Confederate General John Hunt Morgan who twice commandeered the house for use as his headquarters. It was here that the white flag of truce was flown (atop a pole used to clean the tall ceilings) that saved Lebanon from complete destruction by Morgan.

Some time after Spalding's death, the home went to Lucy Cleaver McElroy who was a widely published author and relative of Spalding's wife. One of her novels, *Juletty*, places Morgan's time at Myrtledene into narrative form.

T. C. Jackson, the grandfather of the present owner, purchased the property in 1907 and Myrtledene has been in this family ever since.

Breakfast Sausage with Apples

1 pound fresh link country sausage,
  cut into desired size or leave whole
3 Granny Smith apples, peeled, cored, and sliced
1 small yellow onion, diced
1/2 cup brown sugar
2 tablespoons water

In a large skillet or sauté pan, brown the sausage on all sides on medium-high heat, approximately 10 minutes. Add the apples and onion and cook approximately 10 more minutes. Add brown sugar and water, reduce heat to medium and let simmer until a syrup develops. Simmer until the sausage is fully cooked, approximately 20 minutes.

Yield: 2 servings.

River House Bed and Breakfast

Cheryl and Bernard Cox, Co-Owners
1510 Riverview Drive
Lewisport, Kentucky 42351
270-295-4199, 270-929-0329
Website: www.RiverHouseBnB.com

The River House overlooks the Ohio River, just fifteen miles east of Owensboro, the industrial and cultural hub of western Kentucky. Located along the southern banks of the river, Owensboro is the third largest city in terms of population in Kentucky. It is known as "a city of festivals." Yearly, the world-famous International Bar-B-Q Festival and the Summer Festival draw thousands of spectators and participants from across the country and around the world.

This unique, modern bed and breakfast offers a relaxed atmosphere, beautiful grounds, and private quarters. Enjoy the magnificent evening sunsets from one of four balconies, including one that extends over the riverbank. Escape to a resort-like atmosphere with beautiful flowers and over 100 potted plants, peaceful scenery, and a large in-ground pool. A full country breakfast is often served either pool side or in the spacious sunroom which overlooks the pool and the river.

Watch the hummingbirds, passing boats, and other wildlife from the spacious sunroom. Guests may also bring their own boat or water bike and enjoy access to a boat ramp 300 feet from the bed and breakfast's private dock.

Blueberry French Toast

Toast:

1/2 pound (about 7 slices) French bread, cubed
1 (8-ounce) package cream cheese, diced
1 cup blueberries, fresh or frozen
7 eggs
1 cup milk
1/4 cup maple syrup
3/4 cup chopped pecans

Sauce:

1 cup sugar
2 tablespoons cornstarch
1 cup water
1 cup blueberries, fresh or frozen
1 tablespoon butter
Whipped cream, optional

Place bread cubes in a slightly greased 11 x 7-inch glass baking dish. Sprinkle cream cheese on top of bread cubes and top with blueberries. In a large bowl, beat together eggs, milk, and maple syrup. Pour egg mixture over the bread. Cover baking dish and refrigerate overnight.

The next morning, remove the dish from the refrigerator 30 minutes before baking. Sprinkle the pecans over the mixture before baking. Cover with aluminum foil and bake at 350 degrees for 25 minutes. Uncover the dish and bake for an additional 20 to 25 minutes until golden brown and center is set.

To make the sauce, combine sugar and cornstarch in a saucepan. Add water and boil over medium heat for 3 minutes, stirring constantly. Stir in blueberries and reduce heat, simmer for 8 to 10 minutes, until the berries have burst. Add butter and stir until melted. Serve the sauce in a gravy boat to allow each guest to take as much sauce as they prefer. For an added touch, top with whipped cream.

Yield: 6 servings.

Crescent Roll Apple Dumplings

2 (8-ounce) cans crescent rolls
2 cooking apples, peeled
1 cup sugar
1 1/2 teaspoons cinnamon
2 sticks butter, melted
1 (12-ounce) can of Mountain Dew

Cut each apple into 8 wedges. Wrap each apple wedge in a crescent roll and place in a 9 x 13-inch baking pan. Mix sugar and cinnamon with butter and pour over the apple dumplings. Next pour the Mountain Dew over the dumplings and bake at 350 degrees for 45 minutes.

Yield: 6 to 8 servings.

Scottwood Bed and Breakfast

Timothy and Annette Grahl, Innkeepers
Hwy 421, Leestown Road
PO Box 4370
Midway, Kentucky 40347
877-477-0778 (toll free), 859-846-5037
Website: www.scottwoodbb.com

Built as early as 1795, the house once stood on Ironworks Pike in Scott County. The house was moved in April 1971, to its present location near Midway, in Woodford County. The original wings were rebuilt with an addition to the rear making it a beautiful 9-room country estate. Thus, the new name of Scottwood, reflects both the old and the new locations.

Originally, the brick Federal was a modest tenant house on a farm and modernization through the years was minimal. The beautiful ash floors, the woodwork, the doors and hardware and many built-in cabinets have survived.

The setting of the bed and breakfast is perfect for guests looking for a bit of yesterday. Midway was founded in 1832 and is Kentucky's first railroad town. An active train track is both a centerpiece and a divider of the tiny town's main shopping district. The town's fall festival, held the 3rd weekend in September, is an annual event for many tourists.

The picturesque scenery is some of the most beautiful in the area. Views of neighboring horse farms and the dazzling sunsets by the South Elkhorn Creek, which runs through the five and a half acres of property, await guests. The history of this Kentucky home, the beauty of the gardens, and the anticipation of a scrumptious breakfast will have visitors returning again and again. Scottwood is like coming home.

Grand Morning Glory Croissants

6 croissants
1 cup cranberry-orange marmalade
1/4 cup plus 1 tablespoon orange juice
5 eggs
1 cup heavy cream
1 teaspoon Grand Marnier liqueur
Fresh fruit for garnish

Slice croissants in half. Place bottom half in buttered 9 x 13-inch baking pan. Mix marmalade and orange juice. Put 2 tablespoons aside and spoon remaining mixture over each croissant. Beat eggs, cream, and liqueur until mixed. Place the top portion on each croissant. Gently pour egg/cream mixture over croissants and top with remaining 2 tablespoons of marmalade/orange juice mixture. Cover with plastic wrap and store in the refrigerator overnight. Remove from refrigerator 30 minutes prior to placing in oven. Bake at 350 degrees for 25 minutes. Remove from oven and serve immediately. Garnish with fresh fruit, if desired. Serve with bacon and hash browns.

Yield: 6 (serving size: 1 croissant).

Annette's Homemade Granola

4 cups oats
2 cups wheat germ
1/3 cup sesame seeds
2 cups coconut
1 cup chopped pecans
1 1/2 cups raisins or Craisins
1 cup chopped dates
1/2 teaspoon cinnamon
1/4 teaspoon ground cloves
1/4 teaspoon ginger
1 teaspoon salt
1/2 cup water
3/4 cup light molasses
1/2 cup oil
1 teaspoon vanilla extract (I use Mexican vanilla extract)

Combine first 11 ingredients. Mix liquids and pour over cereal mixture. Mix well. Spread in a large pan and bake at 300 degrees for 40 to 50 minutes, stirring occasionally. Store in an airtight container.

Note: In addition to the above items, I sometimes go to the health food store and choose other nuts, such as almonds, and other ingredients in the bulk food area to add variety to the mixture. It is just as good as is, and is healthy too!

Yield: 2 quarts granola.

Snug Hollow Farm
Bed and Breakfast

Barbara Napier, Innkeeper
790 McSwain Branch
Irvine, Kentucky 40336
606-723-4786
Website: www.snughollow.com

Snug Hollow Farm is nestled in the beautiful Red Lick Valley of Estill County in Central Kentucky just 20 country miles east of Berea, and one hour from Lexington. It is a sanctuary and organic farm that boasts 300 acres of babbling creeks, glorious wildflowers, abundant wildlife, wooded mountainsides, and the simplicity of country life. The area is Appalachia at its best and the chestnut log cabin, with fantastic views, is just a sample.

Guests are invited into a spacious, two-story farmhouse complete with cozy fireplace, charming sunroom filled with quilts, and surrounding roomy porches.

Delicious vegetarian meals of fresh garden produce, as well as hearty breakfasts, tasty lunches, country picnics, and elegant dinners are a culinary delight.

Oatmeal Pancakes

1 cup thick, rolled oats
1 cup all-purpose flour
1/2 cup whole wheat flour
2 1/2 teaspoons baking powder
Pinch of salt
2 large eggs
2 cups buttermilk
5 tablespoons butter, melted
2 tablespoons brown sugar

In a large mixing bowl, combine the dry ingredients and mix well.

In a separate bowl, beat the eggs and stir in the buttermilk, melted butter, and brown sugar. Pour the wet ingredients into the dry ingredients and mix well. Let the mixture sit for 5 minutes and heat the griddle. If the mixture is too dry, add a little more buttermilk.

Coat the griddle with cooking spray to resist sticking and pour 1/2 cup batter for each pancake. Pancakes are generally ready to turn when they first begin to bubble and stiffen on top. For light, fluffy pancakes, refrain from flipping more than once. To serve, heat pure maple syrup and garnish with bananas or blueberries.

Yield: 6 large or 8 small pancakes.

Springhill Winery and Plantation
Bed and Breakfast

Eddie O'Daniel, Innkeeper
3205 Springfield Road
Bloomfield, Kentucky 40008
502-252-9463
Website: www.springhillwinery.com

Located in central Kentucky near Bardstown and historic Bloomfield, Springhill sits on a stately, historic plantation, circa 1857.

Summer visitors often enjoy a play depicting the historic, mysterious events that took place on the plantation in 1864. In the shadow of a huge elm tree, guests enjoy a cool sip of Kentucky's finest wines from Springhill vineyards in addition to an enormous buffet dinner, complete with southern meats, garden vegetables, and desserts.

All rooms have private baths and sitting areas with spectacular views of the rolling hillside. Every morning freshly cut flowers and fresh coffee are delivered to guests. A full country breakfast is served daily at the sprawling brick manor and guests are encouraged to stroll the vineyards, relax in the hammock, and shop in the boutique. Romance and tranquility abound at Springhill.

Baked Plantation Freedom Toast

White bread (stale is fine)
6 to 8 ounces cream cheese, softened
12 to 14 large eggs
1/4 cup half-and-half
1/4 cup maple syrup
3/4 stick butter, melted
Mint, strawberries, confectioners' sugar, and/or
  Kentucky bourbon for garnish

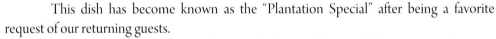

This dish has become known as the "Plantation Special" after being a favorite request of our returning guests.

To prepare, grease a 9 x 13-inch casserole dish and dust with flour. Remove the crust from the bread, and use large pieces to cover the bottom of casserole dish. Spread the cream cheese evenly over bread, not too heavy so that the egg mixture can soak through to the bread. Place another layer of white bread on top of the cream cheese. In a separate bowl, mix eggs, half-and-half, maple syrup, and melted better. Pour mixture over the layers of bread, cover, and refrigerate overnight.

The next morning, bake, uncovered, at 375 degrees for approximately 40 minutes, until the sides and top are nice and brown. If ever you find the middle is not firm, you can remove the dish from the oven and place in the microwave for a couple of minutes on medium power. This is a great way to complete the cooking without burning the top and sides.

I like to add mint garnish with sliced strawberries and sprinkle confectioners' sugar on top. I also mix a little Kentucky bourbon to taste with some buttered maple syrup to pour over the Freedom Toast. It adds a genuine Kentucky touch. Enjoy!

Yield: 8 servings.

English Trifle

Custard Sauce:

1 1/2 tablespoons cornstarch
2 cups light cream, divided
4 large egg yolks, beaten
1/2 cup sugar
1 teaspoon vanilla extract

Layers:

Pound cake, sliced in 1/4-inch slices
3 tablespoons brandy or dry sherry
Jar of seedless raspberry jam
24 coconut macaroons, crumbled
4 cups total crushed pineapples, raspberries,
   bananas, blueberries, and/or strawberries

Topping:

1 to 2 tablespoons confectioners' sugar
2 cups heavy whipped cream
1/2 cup slivered almonds, toasted

In a large mixing bowl, dissolve cornstarch in 1/4 cup light cream. Combine egg yolks with cornstarch mixture. Heat remaining 1 3/4 cups light cream, being careful not to boil, and add sugar, stirring to dissolve. Pour this hot mixture of sweet light cream into the egg yolks, stirring constantly. Return egg mixture to saucepan. Continue to cook over medium heat, stirring until sauce thickens, approximately 5 to 10 minutes. Remove from heat, stir in the vanilla extract, transfer to a bowl, cover with plastic wrap, and cool.

To assemble, in a trifle or other decorative dish, place slices of the pound cake to cover the bottom, sprinkle with brandy (or dry sherry, if you prefer) and spread the seedless raspberry jam on the slices. Cover with a thin layer of macaroons. Top this with layers of the different fruits, as many or few as you wish. Cover this layered fruit with your prepared custard. Repeat layering by starting with the slices of pound cake, macaroons, and fruits as before, and covering with remaining custard.

Do enough layers to fill your dish, then cover and chill for 1 to 2 hours before serving. Add 1 to 2 tablespoons of confectioners' sugar to heavy whipped cream. If using heavy whipping cream, whip cream until stiff peaks form and then add sugar. Add whipped cream as topping along with almonds before serving. It is well worth the time to prepare, enjoy!

Yield: 12 to 14 servings.

Springhill Winery

Springhill Bread Pudding with Old Tawny Port Sauce

This is our classic Springhill Bread Pudding served to impress our morning guests. You can enrich it by using half-and-half instead of milk, add an extra egg, or you can add different fruits, nuts, or Kentucky bourbon.

Bread Pudding:

3 eggs, beaten
1 quart milk
1 loaf French bread
2 cups sugar
1 tablespoon vanilla extract
2 teaspoons ground cinnamon
1 cup raisins
3 tablespoons melted butter
Cinnamon and raisins for top

Old Tawny Port Sauce:

1 stick butter
1 cup sugar
1 egg, beaten
2 ounces (1/4 cup)
   Springhill Old Tawny Port

Whisk the eggs into the milk. Tear bread into chunks and soak in egg mixture. Crush with hands to make sure milk has soaked through. Add sugar, vanilla extract, cinnamon, raisins, and stir well. Pour melted butter into a heavy 9 x 13-inch baking pan to coat the bottom and sides. Add bread mixture and sprinkle more cinnamon and raisins on top and bake at 350 degrees until very firm, approximately 40 minutes. Cool pudding, cube it, and place onto individual dessert dishes.

To prepare sauce, melt butter in a saucepan over low to medium heat and combine remaining ingredients. Stir until entire mixture is blended and warm.

To serve, add Port Sauce and heat under broiler for a few minutes if desired.

Yield: 8 servings.

Swann's Nest

Rosalie Swann, Innkeeper
3463 Rosalie Lane
Lexington, Kentucky 40510
859-226-0095
Website: www.swannsnest.com

A Charter Member of the Kentucky Farm Stays Tourist Trail, Swann's Nest provides guests with an opportunity to experience the Bluegrass in a manner previously enjoyed by only a privileged few. The plantation house, located on a 20-acre farm called Cygnet, is tucked into the rolling countryside, just beyond the back entrance of Keeneland Race Course.

Offering charm, tranquility, and convenience, the location is within minutes of the most prominent central Kentucky thoroughbred and standard-bred horse farms, fine dining, and shopping.

Cold Marinated Asparagus

3/4 small onion, minced
2 teaspoons lemon juice
1 teaspoon salt
1 clove garlic, minced
1/3 cup olive oil
1 1/2 teaspoons red wine vinegar
2 pounds fresh asparagus,
  uniform sized and cleaned
Pimento strips for garnish

In a 9 x 13-inch dish, combine onion, lemon juice, salt, garlic, olive oil, and red wine vinegar and whisk well. In a sauté pan, add water to cover the bottom of the pan and bring water to a boil. Cook or steam the asparagus until tender but still crisp, approximately 3 to 5 minutes; drain. While asparagus is still warm, add asparagus to the marinade in the dish. Cover and refrigerate for 2 to 3 hours. Arrange on a serving plate and garnish with pimento strips for color.

Yield: 6 servings.

Leaf Lettuce with Poppy Seed Dressing

Dressing:

1 teaspoon dry mustard
1 teaspoon salt
1 tablespoon poppy seeds
3/4 cup sugar
1/2 cup apple cider vinegar
1 cup salad oil

Salad:

1 head red leaf lettuce, washed, drained
  and torn into bite-size pieces
1 head green leaf lettuce, washed, drained,
  and torn into bite-size pieces
1 cup sliced strawberries
1 cup canned mandarin oranges

Mix dry dressing ingredients, add vinegar, and then add the oil. Mix well and chill. To serve, assemble salad ingredients in a bowl and pour dressing over the salad.

Yield: 4 servings.

Washington House
Bed and Breakfast

Chuck and Regina Phillips, Owners
283W. 9th Street
Russellville, Kentucky 42276
270-726-1240
Website: www.washingtonhousebb.com

John Whiting Washington, third cousin of George Washington, built the main portion of the house as his townhouse between 1805 and 1824. Thomas Clark purchased the property in 1880, and until 1989, the home remained in the Clark family.

Washington House Bed and Breakfast, circa 1824, is in the historic district of Russellville. The architecture is Colonial Revival in the Federal style. The main portion of the structure has 18-inch thick brick walls and 11-foot ceilings. The front parlor has an original 8-foot wide Adams mantel, flanked by floor to ceiling bookcases. The house is decorated with a mixture of period antiques, artwork, and reproduction furniture.

Grand Ma Jackie's Frozen Salad

1 (8-ounce) can condensed milk
1 (21-ounce) can cherry pie filling
1 (21-ounce) can crushed pineapple, drained
1/2 (16-ounce) package miniature marshmallows
1 (12-ounce) carton whipped cream or heavy cream to be whipped for topping
Chopped walnuts to taste
Lettuce leaves for garnish

In a large bowl, mix the condensed milk and cherry pie filling. Add the pineapple, marshmallows, and whipped cream and mix thoroughly. Spread the mixture into a square or rectangular cake pan, depending upon desired thickness. Sprinkle chopped walnuts on top and place the pan in the freezer until ready to serve. To serve, cut the frozen salad into squares and serve in sherbet glasses or over lettuce leaves on clear glass salad plates.

Yield: 12 to 15 servings; number of servings may vary due to different size containers.

Martha Washington's Excellent Cake

Martha Washington (George's wife) used a cookbook given to her by Frances Park Custis, her deceased first husband's mother, which rated cakes from "a great cake" to "an excellent cake" to "another great cake" or "a great cake, another way" or "a great cake still another way." Although this recipe is around 250 years old, the ingredients are still used today in our baking. In Martha Washington's era, there were no layer cakes; cakes were considered "fruit cakes" which are drier and heavier than our cakes today. Lack of refrigeration meant that foods had to last longer and the drier a cake, the longer it would last. After following the old recipe, I realized that for today's taste, 2 cups of heavy whipping cream and 1/4 cup oil help to make the cake more moist. I also used dried pineapple rather than citron, which is not easy to find in stores today. We do not usually have citron available in the fresh fruit aisle or in the dried fruit or spice section, however it can be ordered online. Citrons are much like lemons but the peel is much fleshier. When processed, it becomes sweeter and is one of the main items in today's store bought fruit cakes.

From *The Martha Washington Cookbook* compiled by Marie Kimball:

1 1/2 cups butter, softened
1 cup sugar
5 eggs, beaten
1 cup cream
   (I suggest 2 cups heavy whipping cream
   and 1/4 cup oil)
4 cups all-purpose flour
1 teaspoon baking soda
1/2 teaspoon salt
1 teaspoon cinnamon
1 teaspoon crushed cloves
   (I suggest using ground cloves)
1 teaspoon mace
2-ounces orange peel, cut fine
2-ounces lemon peel, cut fine
2-ounces citron, cut fine
   (I suggest 4 ounces dried pineapple)
1 1/2 pounds currants

Cream butter well. Add sugar, eggs and cream. Sift the flour with the baking soda, salt, and spices and stir into the first mixture. Finally add the fruits, which have been dusted with flour. Line a tall cake pan (10-inches wide and 5-inches deep) or an angel food cake pan with waxed paper and add the batter. Bake slowly at 275 degrees for 2 hours. Leave plain as Martha did or top with regular cream cheese or lemon frosting to complement the spices in this old and historic cake.

Yield: 8 to 12 servings (serving size: 1 piece).

Kentucky Culinary Heritage

TRUE KY FOOD!

The Kentucky region formed the western part of the wilderness granted to Virginia under the royal charter of 1609. By 1709, hunters began to visit the forests of what is now Eastern Kentucky. These early explorers were known as "long hunters" either because they stayed away months at a time or because they carried long rifles.

When the Cumberland Gap, a pass through the Appalachian Mountains, was discovered in 1750, it opened Kentucky up for exploration and settlement. Daniel Boone passed through the Gap in 1769 and blazed what is now called the Wilderness Road, further opening the Kentucky frontier. A diverse and unique Kentucky cuisine soon began to develop.

"Hunter's Stew," a forerunner to burgoo, was one of the earliest dishes. It was made without a recipe and consisted of whatever choice pieces of meat from freshly killed game were available.

Country Ham and Cream Gravy

submitted by 1840 Tucker House Bed and Breakfast

3 (6-ounce) packages center cut country ham slices, approximately 1/8-inch thick slices
1 quart heavy whipping cream
Biscuits

Lightly spray a 10 x 14-inch baking dish. In a large cast-iron skillet, brown the country ham in batches. Transfer the ham to the prepared baking dish until a single layer is in the bottom. Pour just enough whipping cream over the ham to cover. Continue layering, covering each layer with more whipping cream. When all the ham has been used, pour remaining whipping cream into the skillet with ham drippings and whisk until smooth. Pour over top of casserole. Bake, uncovered, at 275 degrees for 1 hour and 15 minutes or until the country ham is extremely tender. Serve immediately over biscuits or place in a bowl and serve family style with hash brown potatoes or stone-ground grits. This is truly an old Kentucky recipe, handed down from generation to generation for fine Kentucky cooks.

Colonists from Pennsylvania, Virginia, Maryland, North Carolina, and Tennessee were the first white settlements in Kentucky in 1774. They brought basic supplies with them such as cornmeal, salt, smoked ham and bacon, and hard-to-get wheat flour.

Corn was planted and used, not only for food, but to make corn whiskey. Wheat didn't grow well in Kentucky soil so the little they had was saved for special biscuits, pies, and gingerbread for company. Cornmeal was used for most bread and for mush.

Settlers planted vegetables, such as sweet potatoes, carrots, green beans, and okra. Green beans, simmered all day with bacon, were a favorite dish. Eventually these vegetables were added to hunter's stew along with squirrel, possum, rabbit, and meat from birds to create what became known as burgoo. It is comprised of a variety of ingredients, including wild game, pork, beef or lamb and simmered for 24 hours in a large iron pot over open fire.

Like many others, from states settled during the early frontier period, the first pioneers, who called Kentucky home, were presented with challenges. Many of these translated into an eclectic and unique cuisine, reflecting the collective heritage of those hailing from several regions of the globe.

Over the years certain dishes and drinks have become unique to Kentucky. Certainly the mint julep, a heavenly concoction of fine Kentucky bourbon whiskey with fresh mint leaves, is our greatest example. This popular drink has become associated with the greatest two minutes in sports, which takes place every spring in Kentucky. The Kentucky Derby would simply not be complete without this essential drink served to racing fans. Our beloved Kentucky bourbon, first distilled in Bourbon County in 1789, is noted all over the world.

The renowned Derby Pie, created over 50 years ago and now trademarked by Kern's Kitchen, is another tradition enjoyed not only at Derby but at any time during the year. This luscious pie with chocolate chips and nuts has been modified

Benedictine Sandwich Filling

submitted by 1853 Inn at Woodhaven

1 cucumber, peeled
1 small onion
1 (8-ounce) package cream cheese, softened
Salt to taste
Mayonnaise to taste
1 drop green food coloring

Grind cucumber and onion separately, very fine. Place the cucumber and onion in a strainer and press out juice. Add to softened cream cheese. Add salt and mayonnaise and mix well in food processor or with a mixer. Add food coloring and mix again. This filling may be used as a sandwich spread or as a dip with crackers.

Yield: 4 sandwiches.

Recipe on page 32

many times by cooks across the nation in an effort to create an original recipe. Only Alan Rupp, Kern's Kitchen president and grandson of Walter and Leaudra Kern, knows the secret.

Bibb lettuce, created by John B. Bibb who was an amateur horticulturist, is a gourmet delight. This highly prized lettuce, originally called limestone lettuce, has a delicate, sweet flavor. Bibb, who lived in Frankfort, began giving away seeds and plants when he was in his 80s. If not for this act, the wonderful lettuce we often use in our "wilted" recipes would be lost forever.

Over a century ago, a curious recipe evolved called Benedictine. It is named after its creator, Miss Jennie Benedict, a Louisville caterer who provided for many socialite parties. This canapé, sandwich spread, or dip, is well known throughout the Bluegrass and is a must at proper formal teas, cocktail parties, or weddings.

Another name associated with a mainstay on Kentucky tables is Henry Bain. The story goes that Bain, a headwaiter at the exclusive Pendennis Club in Louisville during the 1800s, developed his special sauce for the wild game dishes served by the club. Members liked it so much it was bottled and later sold in local markets. The sauce imparts both the sweet taste of berries or fruit along with a vinegar flavor. Many variations exist; don't be surprised to find this famous Henry Bain Sauce on menus worldwide.

The legendary Hot Brown originated in the Brown Hotel, also in Louisville, in the late 1920s. Chef Fred K. Schmidt created this sandwich that boasts a rich combination of roasted turkey, Mornay sauce, Parmesan cheese, cooked bacon, and pimento atop an open faced, toasted slice of bread. Today the famous dish is prepared by chefs all over the world; Kentuckians can claim fame to this delicious hot sandwich, a signature of the Brown Hotel.

Henry Bain's Sauce

from the Pendennis Club of Louisville, Kentucky
submitted by 1840 Tucker House Bed and Breakfast

1 (12-ounce) bottle chili sauce
1 (14-ounce) bottle ketchup
1 (9-ounce) bottle regular A.1. steak sauce
1 (10-ounce) bottle Worcestershire sauce
2 (9-ounce) bottles Major Grey's Chutney

Mix all ingredients in a blender or use a large bowl and a stick blender to mix. This sauce is frequently used over beef tenderloin and is also a delicious appetizer. Pour over cream cheese and serve with crackers. Enjoy!

Bibb Lettuce Salad with Hot Bacon Dressing

submitted by 1840 Tucker House Bed and Breakfast

1 pound hickory smoked bacon
1/2 cup cider vinegar
1 cup firmly packed brown sugar
6 green onions including tops, chopped
2 tablespoons salt
3 heads Bibb lettuce

Cook the bacon in a skillet. Crumble and set aside, reserving grease. Add the remaining ingredients and stir. Cook until the sugar dissolves. Pour the dressing over Bibb lettuce just before serving.

Yield: 6 servings.

Turkey Hash

submitted by 1853 Inn at Woodhaven

1/2 cup chopped onions
1 stick butter
1/2 cup all-purpose flour
4 cups turkey stock
1/2 teaspoon salt
1/4 teaspoon freshly cracked black pepper
4 cups cooked diced turkey
1/2 cup heavy cream, optional

In a heavy Dutch oven, sauté onions in butter until just softened. Stir in flour and cook over low heat until well blended and bubbly. Slowly add stock, stirring constantly until thickened. Season with salt and pepper and stir in turkey. Simmer 10 minutes and add cream just before serving. Serve over corn cakes; we like to use Weisenberger Mill white cornbread mix.

Yield: 6 to 8 servings.

Hot Brown

submitted by 1853 Inn at Woodhaven

1 stick butter
1 medium onion, minced
1/2 cup all-purpose flour
4 cups hot milk
1 teaspoon salt
Dash of red pepper
Dash of nutmeg
4 egg yolks, slightly beaten
1 cup heavy cream
1 cup grated Parmesan cheese
8 slices quality white bread with crusts trimmed off, toasted
1 turkey breast, cooked and sliced
Extra Parmesan for sprinkling
8 slices quality bacon, cooked thoroughly but not yet crisp

Melt the butter in a large saucepan, add the onion, and sauté for approximately 3 minutes. Stir in the flour and blend using a wire whisk. Add the milk and whisk until blended and smooth. Continue to simmer, stirring frequently, for 20 minutes or until the sauce is thick and smooth. Stir in the salt, red pepper and nutmeg. Cool slightly.

Blend the egg yolks and cream. Add a little of the slightly cooled sauce to the egg yolk mixture and blend. Add this mixture to the saucepan. Add the Parmesan cheese and stir to blend. This can be made the day before and refrigerated.

To assemble the sandwich, place toast in the center of an ovenproof serving dish. Top with turkey slices to cover. Cover completely with the sauce. Sprinkle Parmesan cheese over all. Repeat process using 3 additional plates. Broil at 400 degrees until bubbly and golden brown. Cut a second slice of toast diagonally and put the tip side to the edge of each plate. Crisscross two slices of bacon over each plate.

Yield: 4 servings.

Kentucky Farm Stays

In 2005, the Bed and Breakfast Association of Kentucky introduced a new statewide Agritourism Trail called the "Kentucky Farm Stay." This program was created to encourage Agritourism, which is defined as any business conducted by a farmer for the enjoyment or education of the public, to promote the products of the farm, and to generate additional farm income. It is a way to preserve the family farm and green spaces by opening as a bed-and-breakfast inn. There are a wide variety of farms in which to spend the night, including horse farms, vineyards, fruit orchards, and fiber farms. There is something to offer everyone during any season of the year. Visitors may learn something new such as fiber art, purchase farm products, or take part in farm activities and entertainment.

Tourism ranks as Kentucky's third largest industry, contributing $8.8 billion to the economy, while agriculture earned $4 billion in direct farm gate sales and indirect sales of at least $25 billion. Agritourism is an excellent way to educate the public about the importance of agriculture and its contribution to the economy and quality of life.

Enjoy the experience and beauty of a working Kentucky Farm by staying overnight.

For a complete listing of Kentucky Farm Stays, please visit www.kentuckybb.com or call 1-888-281-8188.

Kentucky Farm Stays

Consumers are looking for quality food products. They increasingly are concerned with what is in their food and where it comes from. And they want to buy their food from down the road rather than across the country or around the globe.

The Kentucky Proud movement has introduced thousands of Kentucky consumers to fresh, nutritious, great-tasting foods from right here in the Commonwealth. Kentucky Proud is the Kentucky Department of Agriculture's marketing program.

"More Kentuckians are finding out what many of us knew all along - when it comes to Kentucky Proud, nothing else is close," Agriculture Commissioner Richie Farmer said. "Kentuckians produce some of the best food you can find anywhere. The Kentucky Department of Agriculture has worked hard to get Kentucky Proud products to the consumer, and our efforts are paying off for Kentucky's farmers."

Kentucky Proud means delicious blackberry jam, rich-tasting Kentucky country ham, mouth-watering fresh tomatoes and much more. The blue, green and red logo that symbolizes Kentucky Proud stands for food products raised or produced in Kentucky by Kentuckians. By late 2007, some 1,000 farmers, processors, retailers, restaurants and farmers' markets were members of Kentucky Proud.

Kentucky Proud generated $39 million in retail sales in 2006, and the 2007 total was expected to be much higher. Kentucky Proud sales to Kentucky state parks exceeded $146,000 in 2006 after the state adopted regulations that allow the parks to buy Kentucky Proud meat and dairy products.

Farmers' markets are popular places for growers to sell their products directly to consumers, and Kentucky Proud is featured prominently in the Commonwealth's 115 markets. Sales at Kentucky farmers' markets were nearly $7 million in 2006, and the number of markets in Kentucky has risen substantially in recent years, reflecting a similar increase nationwide.

When consumers buy local, farmers make more money, and more land stays in farming. Growing support for local foods is driven by consumers' concerns over food safety and their desire to upgrade to better, fresher products.

For more information about Kentucky Proud, go to www.kyproud.com.

Bourbon Mocha

submitted by 1853 Inn at Woodhaven

2 cups heavy whipping cream
1 tablespoon confectioners' sugar
1 tablespoon vanilla extract
2 tablespoons bourbon and
  additional amount to taste
12 cups freshly brewed mocha coffee

Whip cream to soft peaks. Stir confectioners' sugar, vanilla extract, and bourbon into whipped cream. Pour additional bourbon to taste in each cup, add coffee and whipped bourbon cream.

Yield: 10 to 12 servings.

Country Ham and Sausage Patties

submitted by 1853 Inn at Woodhaven

1 pound (ground) cooked country ham
1/2 pound uncooked pork sausage
1 cup dry bread crumbs
1 egg
1 cup milk
1 cup brown sugar
1/2 cup water
1/2 cup white vinegar
1 tablespoon prepared mustard

Combine ham, sausage, bread crumbs, and egg in a large bowl and mix with hands. Slowly add milk, using just enough to make the mixture moist. Roll into balls (recipe can be frozen at this point). When ready to bake, place balls in a single layer in a 10 x 12-inch baking dish.

To prepare sauce, combine sugar, water, vinegar, and mustard in saucepan over medium-high heat. Bring to a boil. Pour sauce over ham balls and bake at 350 degrees for 45 minutes, basting after 25 minutes.

Serve with Auntie Pankie's Garlic Cheese Grits and Red-Eye Gravy.

Yield: 4 dozen.

Red-Eye Gravy

submitted by 1853 Inn at Woodhaven

1 ham steak
Water

In a sauté pan, add water to cover the bottom of the pan. Simmer ham steak in water until water is gone. Lightly brown ham on both sides and remove from pan. Add a little water to the pan drippings and simmer for 3 minutes, stirring constantly.

Serve with Country Ham and Sausage Patties and Auntie Pankie's Garlic Cheese Grits found on page 20.

Nettie Armstrong's Jam Cake

Submitted by 1840 Tucker House Bed and Breakfast

1 cup (2 sticks) butter
2 cups sugar
1/2 cup dark brown sugar
8 egg yolks, stirred
4 cups all-purpose flour
1 tablespoon cinnamon
1 teaspoon cloves
1 teaspoon nutmeg
1/8 teaspoon salt
8 egg whites
1 teaspoon baking soda
1 cup buttermilk
32 to 36 ounces blackberry jam
1 cup raisins, optional
1 cup chopped walnuts or pecans, optional

Caramel Icing for Jam Cake:

3/4 cup (1 stick) butter
1 1/2 cups firmly packed dark brown sugar
3/4 cup plus 2 tablespoons half-and-half
1/2 teaspoon salt
6 cups or more to taste sifted confectioners' sugar

To prepare the cake, grease 4 (9-inch) cake pans and line with parchment paper. Grease parchment paper and set pans aside.

In a large bowl, cream butter until fluffy; add sugars gradually and cream until light and fluffy. Add stirred egg yolks and beat well. In a separate large bowl, whisk together the flour, cinnamon, cloves, nutmeg, and salt. If using nuts and raisins, save a bit of the flour mixture to dredge the nuts and raisins together. Slowly add the dry mixture to the creamed mixture. In a separate deep bowl, beat the egg whites, taking care that they are not too stiff! Fold the whites into the batter. In a small bowl, dissolve baking soda into the buttermilk and set aside.

Add the jam, buttermilk/soda mixture, raisins, and nuts to the batter. Carefully pour batter into the prepared pans, taking care to ensure the amounts in each pan are even; a kitchen scale is helpful in this step. Bake at 350 degrees for approximately 20 to 25 minutes or until a wooden pick inserted into the center of one of the layers comes out moist, but clean. Start testing at 20 minutes, as you do not want this cake to over-bake!

Cool pans on wire racks for 10 minutes. Turn the cake out of the pans onto wire racks and allow the cakes to cool to room temperature before icing with caramel icing.

To prepare icing, combine the first four ingredients in a heavy saucepan. Cook over medium heat until mixture comes to a boil, stirring constantly. Boil 2 minutes. Remove from heat and cool mixture to 160 degrees. Beat in confectioners' sugar until icing is of spreadable consistency. Ice quickly, because icing will begin to harden the longer it sits. Enjoy!

Yield: 20 servings.

Index

Cookbook Committee   From left to right: Marsha Burton, 1853 Inn at Woodhaven; Cindy McDavid; Nancy Hinchliff, Aleksander House Bed and Breakfast; Nancy Swartzel, Burlington's Willis Graves Bed and Breakfast Inn; Carol Stenbro, Market Street Inn; and Devona Porter, 1840 Tucker House Bed and Breakfast.

Robin Victor Goetz, M.Photog.Cr., is well known for a unique perspective and style in residential, commercial, and industrial environments. Creative angles and a unique flair for catching everyday subjects in a dramatic light have helped Robin to fast become one of the most in-demand photographers in the Midwest.

Born, raised, and currently living in Northern Kentucky, Robin is a true Kentucky product. After graduating in 1983 from Scott High School in Taylor Mill, Robin immediately began taking photography classes and assisting local prominent photographers. By late 1984, the call of travel and adventure beckoned, and Robin entered the U.S. Navy. Within 11 months, he had captured the coveted title of being a U.S. Navy Official Photographer aboard the USS John F. Kennedy CV-67 aircraft carrier. Robin's ability to photograph a wide variety of subjects no doubt came from his duties as Ship's Photographer. During his navy stint, Robin had the honor of photographing a past President and First Lady, multiple celebrities (including Bob Hope and Brooke Shields) and many foreign Heads of State. He earned the opportunity to travel across Europe and the Middle East to photograph for official U.S. Navy publications.

Robin graduated from the Ohio Institute of Photography with photographic degrees in portraiture, commercial, and corporate in 1991. Later that same year he received his Certified Professional Photographer certification from the Professional Photographers of America (PPA). In 1993, Robin was awarded his master of photography degree with his photographic craftsman degree being awarded a short 2 years later, both by the PPA.

Robin has taught professional photography at the Antonelli Institute of Art and Photography and his Alma Mater, now the Ohio Institute of Photography and Technology. He has also conducted hundreds of workshops and lectures across the nation.

In 1995, Robin Victor Goetz Photography (RVGP) was instituted and continues today. The year 2008 marks Robin's 25th year of providing photographic excellence.

Robin Victor Goetz may be reached through his web site at www.GoRVGP.com or 859-431-8400.

Robin Goetz
5387 Shadow Hill Ct.
Taylor Mill, KY 41015
859-431-6730 Home
859-431-8400 Office
RVGP@insightbb.com
www.GoRVGP.com